To: Lucas

MW01059425

city craigslist > items wanted

Wanted: Bear Cubs for My Children

Reply to: sale-0005DXS060603@craigslist.org
Date: 2007-09-17, 5:34PM PST

One Hundred of the Weirdest Posts Ever Seen on Craigslist (and Their Responses)

- Location:America
- it's NOT ok to contact this poster with services or other commercial interests

PostingID: Gary Fingercastle

adamsmedia

Avon, Massachusetts

Published by
Adams Media, a division of F+W Media, Inc.
57 Littlefield Street, Avon, MA 02322. U.S.A.
www.adamsmedia.com

ISBN 10: 1-60550-357-6
ISBN 13: 978-1-60550-357-8

Printed in the United States of America.

J   I   H   G   F   E   D   C   B   A

Library of Congress Cataloging-in-Publication Data
is available from the publisher.

This publication is designed to provide accurate and authoritative information
with regard to the subject matter covered. It is sold with the understanding that
the publisher is not engaged in rendering legal, accounting, or other professional
advice. If legal advice or other expert assistance is required, the services of a
competent professional person should be sought.

—From a *Declaration of Principles* jointly adopted by a Committee of the
American Bar Association and a Committee of Publishers and Associations

Many of the designations used by manufacturers and sellers to distinguish their
product are claimed as trademarks. Where those designations appear in this book
and Adams Media was aware of a trademark claim, the designations have been
printed with initial capital letters.

This book is available at quantity discounts for bulk purchases.
For information, please call 1-800-289-0963.

Contents

Chapter 4: Dating 85

Chapter 5: Free Stuff 109

Chapter 6: For Sale 163

Chapter 7: Barter 173

Chapter 8: Movies 181

Chapter 9: Random 195

Chapter 10: Flagged 209

An open letter to the craigslist community

Dear Craigslist Users,

I do not want pictures of your penises. Throughout the course of writing *Wanted: Bear Cubs for My Children*, I did not once ask you for pictures of your penises. Sure, I asked if you would dress up like a Christmas tree and have sex with me. I asked if you would give my twelve year old daughter a tattoo. I even asked if you would take my infant skydiving. But through it all, I made a very cognizant effort not to ask for pictures of your penises. And yet, there they were. Thousands of them. Digital penises overflowing my inbox. Circumcised penises. Mutated penises. Crushed penises. Penises with candles in them.

You thought your penis trick was so clever, didn't you? You probably sat at your desk, laughing while you took pictures of your penis and sent them to me. You imagined me opening your email and spitting coffee all over my monitor, shocked at the sight of your deformed member. Then, you probably patted yourself on the back and thought, "Wow. That was a funny trick." You prankster, you.

Well, I suppose I'll accept your apology, if you'll accept mine. You see, in the end, I'm the real prankster. Over the past several years, I've posted hundreds of fake ads on craigslist, posing as hundreds of different people, and received tens of thousands of replies. I altered my grammar and misspelled my words to convince you that I was real. I had you begging for my reply. I had you in the palm of my hand. I studied you for months. I memorized your every nuance. I learned your lingo and your methodology. I transformed myself and became one of you.

It's time for me to come clean with you, craigslist community. I'm not a Methodist minister. I'm not a crazy cat woman. I'm not a wealthy philanthropist, a dominatrix, a scientist, or a murderer. And I'm certainly not a meth addict. I'm just a writer with a sense of humor and an imagination. If I've let any of you down, take consolation in the fact that it was a treat compiling this book. You surprised me at every turn.

See, I never thought you'd be up for some casual sex in a lion's cage. Call me crazy, but I think that's just downright reckless. I never thought you'd pay to see a donkey fight. I never thought you'd pose as a robber and break into my apartment. I never thought you'd want a book covered in human skin or a dinosaur skeleton. And I never thought you'd send me pictures of your penises. But you did. And you won my heart in the process.

You're an amazing bunch, craigslist community. You'll do anything to have sex. You'll use balloons, animal costumes, leather and sandwich makings. You agreed, at different points, to date an insane elderly woman, a Klanswoman, and a psychotic shut-in. You promised to dress up like Roseanne Barr for my enjoyment. Wow.

Also, you really, really wanted to pee on me.

I need to give credit where credit is due. I never thought you'd want an armoire covered in blood and pentagram-carvings. But after reading through your five hundred replies, I realized something. You want anything, so long as it's free. *Star Wars* figurines covered in dog feces? You'll take them, no questions asked. An antique mirror with an ancient curse? No problem. A used dildo? You bet.

In fact, I had a hard time coming up with something that you wouldn't take off my hands. After you offered to pick up a mummy, a urine-soaked chair, an evil doll and a Pauly Shore cutout, I gave up. You were truly insatiable. You wanted it all, and you wanted it for free. And your appetite for material goods didn't end there. You were willing to trade your wife's underwear for a video game console. You offered to scour the scene of a meth lab explosion for a few DVDs. And every job I posted—be it for human crash test dummies or actors for the fictitious film *Werewolf Warriors*—received scores of replies. The only ones that didn't were those flagged and removed before you had the chance to respond.

Craigslist community, I have peered into the abyss of your collective consciousness and seen your naked core. I have connected with your innermost desires through blankets of anonymity and inspired action and emotion in you. I have carved a digital everyman out of email blocks and sutured postings. He has your face; it is a face pockmarked with the remnants of pre-digital man. It is the face of our burgeoning America.

You represent the future of human interaction. Your social patterns are unprecedented and your lack of inhibition is startling. Behind your computer screen, you are fearless and anonymous. You are the new generation of consumers, thinkers, entertainers, and poets. Your behavior is irrational and absurd.

You frighten me. But you inspire me, too, with your generosity, your wit, and your sheer, up-for-anything zeal for life. So thank you, craigslist community. Thank you for providing me with some of the strangest, most enjoyable years of my life.

A Note on the Text

What follows is a collection of posts made on craigslist by Gary Fingercastle and their real replies. The author, in many cases, has purposefully added misspellings and infelicities of grammar to properly blend in with the online community. Aside from personal information—which has been blacked out— all content is presented in full, as it was posted, and as it was received.

Chapter 1: Animal Issues

Purchasing bear cubs for children, selling tickets to a donkey fight, and offering a monkey butler up for adoption—these are a few things you'll encounter in the following chapter. I learned several valuable lessons while compiling these pages: ticket sales for donkey fights are sluggish and people are less likely to adopt pets mutated by mad scientists than those not mutated by mad scientists. Also, if a horse is loose in your apartment, call animal control instead of posting your predicament on craigslist.

please flag with care:
miscategorized
prohibited
spam/overpost
best of craigslist

Wanted: Bear Cubs - $100

Reply to: sale-397208395@craigslist.org
Date: 2007-08-14, 5:21PM PDT

My wife and I, after years of nagging, have decided to give our children what they really want: a bear cub. We feel the bear will teach them many important lessons about life and will be a perfect guardian. We're willing to spend upwards of one hundred dollars on a bear and we have plenty of room in our three bedroom apartment since my cousin Wayne moved out.

Please help us make this happen. My children will thank you!

* it's NOT ok to contact this poster with services or other commercial interests

PostingID: 397208395

To: sale-397208395@craigslist.org
Subject: WANTED: Bear Cubs - $100
Date: Tue, 14 Aug 2007 21:12:08 -0700
From: ███████████████

you must be totally joking! well i hope you are anyways. the only lesson i am sure that your children will learn is that bears dont belong in apartments, wildlife and game conservation officers will probably arrest you as soon as you are seen with it. do you think that would be a good lesson to learn for them. please why are you encouraging people to go out and get you a bear for profit. do some research.

To: sale-397208395@craigslist.org
Subject:
Date: Wed, 15 Aug 2007 00:36:07 +0000
From: ███████████████

i will sell you a bear cub for 99.99

email this posting to a friend

please flag with care:
miscategorized
prohibited
spam/overpost
best of craigslist

We're havin us a donkey fight – Tickets on sale NOW! - $5

Reply to: sale-454863273@craigslist.org
Date: 2007-10-20, 5:27PM CDT

Next Saturday down at my buddy Jake's farm, we're havin us a donkey fight. Jake's raised these asses to be MEAN sons a bitches and theyre thirsty for BLOOD! Theres a brown one that we call Blackie whos so pissed he chewed through a god damned electrical fence. Then, theres the black one that we call Beansie, whos big as a horse and MEAN! Come watch these burros brawl it out in a balls-to-the-wall FREE FOR ALL!!!

Tickets for the fight are five dollars and include access to the keg.

* it's NOT ok to contact this poster with services or other commercial interests

PostingID: 454863273

To: sale-454863273@craigslist.org
Subject: We're havin us a donkey fight – Tickets on sale NOW! - $5
Date: Sat, 20 Oct 2007 19:42:15 -0500
From: ▮▮▮▮▮▮▮▮▮▮▮▮

Hey! Tell me where. I'm there! Sounds like fun.

[4 | Wanted: Bear Cubs for My Children]

email this posting to a friend

please flag with care:
miscategorized
prohibited
spam/overpost
best of craigslist

Horse loose in apartment... help!

Reply to: comm-505527641@craigslist.org
Date: 2007-12-11, 12:04AM CST

Two months ago, I left my husband of twelve years and moved into a loft of my own. We shared a farm together prior to the separation. This evening, I came home from work to find my prized horse Peanut running circles around my living room. Since then, he's fallen through my coffee table, eaten my houseplants, pooped all over my carpet and bitten me (twice). I can't calm him down! Every time I get near him, he runs full speed around the living room, down the hallway, over my bed, and back around to the kitchen. My neighbors have threatened to call the cops!

Is there anything I can do to stop him? So far I've tried feeding him carrots, petting him, singing to him and dancing for him. I even played some Doobie Brothers and lit scented candles—nothing! Should I buy a pistol? Should I open my door and let him run free? I love Peanut, but he's ruining my evening!

My husband put him here for a reason. This reason is because I cheated on him. Should I sue my husband?

What do I do?

* it's NOT ok to contact this poster with services or other commercial interests

PostingID: 505527641

To: comm-505527641@craigslist.org
Subject: Horse loose in apartment... help!
Date: Tue, 11 Dec 2007 6:17:57 -EST
From: ▓▓▓▓▓▓▓▓▓▓▓▓

Either call a vet or call animal control. The animal has been fed something to act this way or was the animal this way before you left your husband?

To: comm-505527641@craigslist.org
Subject: Horse loose in apartment... help!
Date: Tue, 11 Dec 2007 09:25:08 -0600
From: ▓▓▓▓▓▓▓▓▓▓▓▓

This must be a joke. But if it is real you really need to find a place for the horse, or dog or whatever it is.

please flag with care:
miscategorized
prohibited
spam/overpost
best of craigslist

Mutated cat needs a good home

Reply to: comm-454820107@craigslist.org
Date: 2007-10-20, 5:31PM EDT

I've recently conducted a series of experiments on test animals from my basement laboratory and compiled startling data. Beginning with mice, I mutated genes and grafted ligaments in an attempt to produce super strength and endurance. I developed a gelatinous compound which, when ingested, resulted in unprecedented mutations in control amphibians and insects. Last Thursday, my Calico cat got into the lab, ate the gelatinous compound, and mutated.

Since Thursday, she's grown to six times her normal size and developed an extreme sensitivity to electromagnetic waves. She's also grown an additional tail and an extra set of teeth. She's had an insatiable appetite and developed the musculature to run at super-speeds.

She's free to a loving home.

* it's NOT ok to contact this poster with services or other commercial interests

PostingID: 454820107

To: comm-454820107@craigslist.org
Subject: Mutated cat needs a good home
Date: Sat, 20 Oct 2007 18:20:53 -0400
From: ███████████████

Awesome, dude

████████████████████
███████████
████████████
██████████████
███████████████████

Monkey Butler up for Adoption

Reply to: comm-gcsqt-1240177006@craigslist.org
Date: 2009-06-25, 9:02PM PDT

I have a money butler in need of a good home. I've trained him to serve appetizers, answer the door, bring breakfast in bed, skateboard, cartwheel, whistle, and swim. He's also a very talented drummer.

I no longer require his services.

He comes with three tuxedos and a pair of white gloves.

* it's NOT ok to contact this poster with services or other commercial interests

PostingID: 1240177006

To: comm-gcsqt-1240177006@craigslist.org
Subject: Monkey
Date: Friday, June 26, 8:19 PM
From: ████████████████

I would love to adopt the butler, but was wondering if he got along with other pets such as dogs?

Thank you

████████████████

To: comm-gcsqt-1240177006@craigslist.org
Subject: Monkey Butler up for Adoption
Date: Friday, June 26, 4:48 PM
From: ████████████████

Im interested my husband wants a monkey, if you're serious i would love more info! Thanks and God bless!

To: comm-gcsqt-1240177006@craigslist.org
Subject: Monkey Butler up for Adoption
Date: Friday, June 26, 4:49 AM
From: ████████████████

Shut the fuck up. please excuse me. are u kidding me. I have always dreamed this day would happen good things so come to good people.

I will tke such good care of monkey butler!!!!!

p.s. i love tuxedos! we can match!

Chapter 2: Job Opportunity

Dear Everyone Who Wants Money,

Searching for jobs online is overwhelming. I understand your frustrations. The competition is high, and positions are limited. But no matter how bad the economy gets, careers that include the following in their job descriptions:

Beating shit up.
Crashing cars into walls at high speeds.
Giving children tattoos.
Starving for six weeks.

. . . are not real. Something to remember for your next job hunt.

please flag with care:
miscategorized
prohibited
spam/overpost
best of craigslist

Department of Car Safety Seeking Paid Volunteers

Reply to: gigs-45854064@craigslist.org
Date: 2007-10-20, 3:16PM MST

We are attempting to assess the safety of a new line of Minivans, and are seeking to move beyond crash test dummies in our assessment. Thus, we are looking to hire six paid volunteers to ride in these vehicles and endure several high-speed impacts. Eligible candidates will work closely with our design and safety team for four weeks, during which they will participate in some 300 collisions.

Payment for the four weeks is set at $50,000.

* it's NOT ok to contact this poster with services or other commercial interests

PostingID: 45854064

[12 | Wanted: Bear Cubs for My Children]

To: gigs-454854064@craigslist.org
Subject: Department of Car Safety Seeking Paid Volunteers
Date: Sat, 20 Oct 2007 20:26:59 -0700
From: ▓▓▓▓▓▓▓▓▓▓▓▓▓▓

sounds like i,m the one 4 this job
i,m ready to go LETS DO THIS
I,M 4 REASL

▓▓▓▓▓▓▓▓▓▓▓▓▓▓▓▓▓

glendale az

To: gigs-454854064@craigslist.org
Subject: Department of Car Safety Seeking Paid Volunteers
Date: Sat, 20 Oct 2007 21:18:05 -0700
From: ▓▓▓▓▓▓▓▓▓▓▓▓

▓▓▓▓▓▓▓▓▓▓▓▓▓▓▓

Sounds scary but also well paying. What are the chances of Dying? My # is
▓▓▓▓ Please call me and let me know more about it

To: gigs-454854064@craigslist.org
Subject: crash test humans
Date: Sat, 20 Oct 2007 14:38:30 -0700
From: ▓▓▓▓▓▓▓▓▓▓▓

is there any medical help available in addition to the payment? just in case of a
broken something. also, has there been another crash test human test before?

email this posting to a friend

Handyman needed to get Grandpa out of the walls

Reply to: <u>serv-451394541@craigslist.org</u>
Date: 2007-10-16, 9:37PM PDT

My father was digging around in our attic last Saturday and he somehow managed get stuck in between our living room wall and our brick siding. Yesterday, we heard him walking around the inside of our kitchen walls, grumbling to himself and tapping on the support beams. Last night, my wife heard him somewhere near the guest bathroom, singing a song in Yiddish. I've tried to talk to him but he can't hear me. We need a handyman to come over and help us get him out of there before he hurts himself.

Name your price.

* it's NOT ok to contact this poster with services or other commercial interests

PostingID: 451394541

[14 | Wanted: Bear Cubs for My Children]

To: serv-451394541@craigslist.org
Subject: Handyman needed to get Grandpa out of the walls
Date: Tue, 16 Oct 2007 22:36:06 -0700 (PDT)
From: ████████████████

Demo work- 100,000 an hour...

Dry wall work to fix the demo 300 an hour...

Kitchen remodel to find him in the walls- depends on the upgrades you will want...

Beam work that grandpa damaged by tapping on them will need to be evaluated...

Guest bathroom will depend on upgrades you want...

To listen to your grandpa sing in yiddish....priceless!

email this posting to a friend

please flag with care:
miscategorized
prohibited
spam/overpost
best of craigslist

Wanted: A Tattoo Artist for my Daughter

Reply to: sale-410286054@craigslist.org
Date: 2007-08-30, 8:36PM CDT

My daughter wants to get a tattoo she drew of Cathy from the Cathy comics swimming with the Little Mermaid. Thing is, she's only twelve. I dont care and her mother dont care (because her mother's long gone), but we cant find an artist to do it around here.

I'll give you a couple hundred bucks, maybe more. Just something small on her shoulder. Shes been bugging me about it for a year now

* it's NOT ok to contact this poster with services or other commercial interests

PostingID: 410286054

To: sale-410286054@craigslist.org
Subject: Wanted: A Tattoo Artist for my Daughter
Date: Thu, 30 Aug 2007 20:39:41 -0700 (PDT)
From: ████████████████

LADY WHAT THE HELL IS WRONG WITH YOU SHE IS ONLY 12 DO"NT LET CPS GET OF HOLD OF YOU I WORK FOR THE DEPT I WILL TURN YOU IN.

To: sale-410286054@craigslist.org
Subject: Wanted: A Tattoo Artist for my Daughter
Date: Thu, 30 Aug 2007 21:22:08 -0500
From: ████████████████

have you tried ████████████ on ████████ Rd? They did quite a few for my son and
they are great –

email this posting to a friend

Hiring Test Subjects - $5,000

Reply to: job-nwxd7-1084448261@craigslist.org
Date: 2009-03-20, 7:32PM EDT

At the Ann Arbor Center for Neuropathology and Brain Studies, we are holding tests throughout the month of April on the human pain threshold. Candidates must be drug free and between the ages of 21 and 45. Subjects will take part in a combination of the following experiments while outfitted in a neurocap:

1.) Needles in forehead.
2.) Hot water on genitals.
3.) Spider bites on neck and back.
4.) Blunt trauma to stomach and kneecaps.
5.) Rope whippings on arms and legs.
6.) "The Treatment"
7.) "The Works"
8.) Cigarette burns on buttocks
9.) Bamboo lashings on abdomen
10.) Scrotal scratching and pinching

The study pays $5,000 a week and includes liquid meals, nightly sedatives, and sauna access.

* it's NOT ok to contact this poster with services or other commercial interests

PostingID: 1084448261

[18 | Wanted: Bear Cubs for My Children]

To: job-nwxd7-1084448261@craigslist.org

Subject: Hiring Test Subjects - $5,000

Date: Fri, 20 Mar 2009 11:46 PM

From: ████████████████

I'm interested in this study would like to know what I need to do to take part.
Thank You

████████████████████

email this posting to a friend

Hiring lazy, unmotivated manager

Reply to: job-454839859@craigslist.org
Date: 2007-10-20, 3:56PM MDT

I would like to hire a lazy, piece of shit manager for my ███████ store. My previous lazy, piece of shit managers have worked out well. You would ideally be unmotivated, sarcastic, unpunctual and impolite to my regular customers. Applicants must have two of the following qualities:

* a drug addiction
* anger issues
* kleptomania
* cancer
* undisciplined children
* a motorcycle

Salary is set at a rate lower than you want, so that you can bitch all the time about how you're not getting paid enough. Hours go late into the night on the weekends and early on weekdays, so that it is impossible for you to get an adequate amount of sleep. There is no room for advancement.

Please reply with a resume and a cover letter about yourself.

* Compensation: less than you think
* Principals only. Recruiters, please don't contact this job poster.
* Please, no phone calls about this job!
* Please do not contact job poster about other services, products or commercial interests.

PostingID: 454839859

[20 | Wanted: Bear Cubs for My Children]

To: job-454839859@craigslist.org
Subject: Hiring lazy, unmotivated manager
Date: Sat, 20 Oct 2007 18:47:37 EDT
From: ███████████

Hi...

You're in luck... I believe I am the "lazy piece of shit manager" you are looking for!

Not only am I sarcastic, I can be downright rude, although I do have a soft spot for children (under 5 only) and elderly adults (over 70 only). Unfortunately, I can be "motivated" and "punctual", but I can certainly "tone" these unwanted traits down... especially if you are around. I did have an undisciplined child, but she grew up to be a pretty amazing woman. I do, however, have an undisciplined dog... will that redeem me in any way?

I also have some unresolved anger issues that stem from my childhood, so the chances of those ever being resolved are zero to none, however, I have learned to place a "white bubble of light" around myself, when I feel as though I'm beginning to slide down that slippery slope of rage, which helps somewhat (although most conditions must be perfect, i.e.; moon and stars in alignment, no current outbreaks on my face, and no embarrassing problems with my elimination system).

And as far as a low salary, I'm used to that, and I'm used to bitching about that too. But hey, I'll even bitch is the salary is better than average! Oh, and don't worry about me not getting enough sleep... I usually have an insomnia problem and do the lion's share of any work I have then!

I don't know about you, but this sounds like a "match made in heaven"... what do you think?

Patiently awaiting your response...

███████████████

To: job-454839859@craigslist.org
Subject: Hiring lazy, unmotivated manager
Date: Sat, 20 Oct 2007 20:36:09 EDT
From:

Interesting post.

Dear Sirs,

I have over 20 years management experience in the restaurant industry.
I have successfully managed various types of concepts from Full Serve Family dining, fast food,   to Quick Serve to take Out & Delivery. I have been able to achieve positive sales
trends in almost every case.
I feel that I have a lot to offer your company and would like a chance to discuss it with you.

please flag with care:
miscategorized
prohibited
spam/overpost
best of craigslist

Will you make shock collars for my children?

Reply to: serv-451387154@craigslist.org
Date: 2007-10-17, 12:26AM EDT

I have three children aged 7, 9, and 12, that will not listen to a word I say. They're always spilling shit everywhere and they won't ever shut their mouths. Sometimes, they even ask me to buy them candy or a toy, knowing that I don't have a job. The oldest one is always hitting the middle one and the youngest one has a bedwetting problem. I feel like I've tried everything. I need three shock collars, and I'm willing to give you my last tax return for them.

This way, they won't run from me and they won't talk back. I can teach the youngest one to stop pissing the bed. And best of all, I can leave them home alone without having to worry about them making a mess.

* it's NOT ok to contact this poster with services or other commercial interests

PostingID: 451387154

To: serv-451387154@craigslist.org
Subject: Will you make shock collars for my children?
Date: Wed, 17 Oct 2007 18:49:16 -0700 (PDT)
From: ████████████████

Here is an idea for you. You should have a shock collar made for yourself. That way every time you realize that you are a horrible parent you can shock yourself. Good luck loser!

To: serv-451387154@craigslist.org
Subject: Will you make shock collars for my children?
Date: Wed, 17 Oct 2007 06:50:55 -0400
From: ████████████████

Try hiring a disciplinarian to spank them good once in awhile, lol.

email this posting to a friend

Seeking someone to live my life for six months

please flag with care:
miscategorized
prohibited
spam/overpost
best of craigslist

Reply to: gigs-454824259@craigslist.org
Date: 2007-10-20, 2:36AM PDT

I am looking to hire a white male, aged 35, with short brown hair and a stocky build, to live my life for the next six months. Compensation is $50,000. You will go to work for me, live in my house, sleep in the same bed as my wife, and discipline my children. Applicants must only partially resemble me. It doesn't really matter. No one pays attention anyway.

I'll give you a long list of things to remember. You will have access to my gym, country club, and Lakers season tickets. You will go to work Monday-Friday, 9am to 5pm, at an accounting firm. I've already done all the work ahead of time, so all you will really have to do is sit behind my desk and nod at people.

I will be taking a break from my life and will be unreachable.

Please reply with a bit about yourself and a photograph.

* it's NOT ok to contact this poster with services or other commercial interests
* Compensation: $50,000

PostingID: 454824259

To: gigs-454824259@craigslist.org
Subject: Seeking someone to live my life for six months
Date: Sun, 21 Oct 2007 18:18:06 EDT
From: ███████████████

Do you pay 25k at first and the rest after 6 months?

To: gigs-454824259@craigslist.org
Subject: Seeking someone to live my life for six months
Date: Sat, 20 Oct 2007 17:05:13 -0700
From: ███████████████

I'm not going to lie...I'm only 23...I look a bit older, but not 35. However, I am extremely intrigued by this post. I would love to hear more. If you would consider someone significantly younger - I'm interested.

Best-

--

█████████

████████████

To: gigs-454824259@craigslist.org
Subject: Seeking someone to live my life for six months
Date: Sat, 20 Oct 2007 16:19:43 -0700
From: ███████████████

Ok were do I sign and is this a good way to really get peoples emails to spam. Wire 10 grand into my account and we can discuss the rest.
Regards,

[26 | Wanted: Bear Cubs for My Children]

To: gigs-454824259@craigslist.org
Subject: This is MY job!!!
Date: Sun, 21 Oct 2007 15:05:45 -0700 (PDT)
From: ███████████████

Hi, This reminds me of the movie "Trading Places";

You are obviously very successful (at least, financially) and I am flat broke. Literally. You have a wife and kids, I'm single w/ no current prospects for a girlfriend (because I'm broke).

You have a career, I'm an out of work actor (w/ no agent) so, no real possibilities of work on the horizon.

The good news is I always have the tendancy to be drawn to new challenges and unique experiences. This would be perfect for both of us. Because as much as you want my life ("no worries"), I want yours.

If you want to see some pics, go to ███████████████████████████

If you want to talk, my number is ████████████

I'm just wondering how your wife would react???? Don't you think she will move out?

███████████████

I'll pay you to hang out with me

Reply to: sale-454846110@craigslist.org
Date: 2007-10-20, 5:05PM CDT

Just because I'm a shut in doesn't meen i cant have any friends. So heres all about me:

37 years old
Still live with the parents
Work at the Taco Bell
Love Star Trek, Warcraft, Everquest, Magic and Xbox360
Big

Im not asking for a girlfriend or anything, I just want for someone to come over and hang out with me for a couple of hours and I'll give you fifty bucks. We could play my Xbox, watch my mom's Trek cassettes or go swimming. Im a pretty nice guy. Pretty lonely, though.

My last friend Turk stopped hanging out with me because he said i was too weird for him and this girl Cassandra was coming around for a while but she hated all the pet rats I got so she stopped calling me. My dads a drunk too, so that didn't help. Hes pretty racist but that shouldn't be a problem.

Lets hang out with me for fifty bucks.

* it's NOT ok to contact this poster with services or other commercial interests

PostingID: 454846110

To: sale-454846110@craigslist.org
Subject:
Date:
From: ███████████████████

if you want to "pay" someone to hang out with you then you should call and hang out
with me ███████ horny ask for ██████

To: sale-454846110@craigslist.org
Subject: I'll pay you to hang out with me
Date: Sat, 20 Oct 2007 18:52:02 -0500
From: ████████████████

I know nothing about any of things you are interested in, but I had to email you a
reply because you made me laugh. Don't worry you are not the only 37 year old
that I know of who still lives with his parents, so I don't really find that to be strange.
I myself am 30 and spent about 6 months with mine, due to homelessness. People
think I am wierd because I talk about all kinds of strange things and, even though I
am damn cute, guys are mostly just afraid of me. I can't hang out with you because
I actually live too far away but if you want an interesting email friend, I volunteer. My
name is ████████

email: ████████████████████

P.S. why are you a shut-in??

email this posting to a friend

My nine year old son needs a job

Reply to: serv-451371272@craigslist.org
Date: 2007-10-16, 9:04PM PDT

To help me pay for his child support. Shit's through the roof and I don't want to work a full time job. So I figure, if he gets a part time job and I work my job at Arby's, we'll have enough to make his mother happy. And I'll be able to watch my TV and maybe get working on those puzzles I bought last April.

He's pretty strong and he can run really fast. I think he'd be good for hauling or any labor work. He goes to school until three every day, but after that, he's good to go.

* it's NOT ok to contact this poster with services or other commercial interests

PostingID: 451371272

To: pers-451371272@craigslist.org
Subject: My nine year old son needs a job
Date: Wed, 17 Oct 2007 10:33:58 EDT
From: ▇▇▇▇▇▇▇▇▇▇▇▇

Hey dead beat try getting a second job and quit making your son work at nine years old ! Im sure someone from the county would like to see this posting you have, so I will forward this page to them-

[30 | Wanted: Bear Cubs for My Children]

email this posting to a friend

please flag with care:
miscategorized
prohibited
spam/overpost
best of craigslist

Adult Volunteers needed for health tests

Reply to: job-454851380@craigslist.org
Date: 2007-10-20, 6:11PM EDT

We are seeking adult volunteers to participate in a study on the effects of prolonged starvation when combined with experimental eating supplements. Potential candidates will have a clean bill of health, will be non-smokers, and will be between the ages of 21 and 40. Candidates will be screened for the use of illegal substances.

Chosen volunteers will live at the hospital, in closed and monitored quarters, for six weeks. During the first five weeks, volunteers will be given no food and will be monitored for metabolic changes. Thereafter, volunteers will be given injections of experimental eating supplements and monitored.

Given the nature of these test, compensation is set at $100,000. Candidates will go through a series of tests and interviews before being declared eligible.

* it's NOT ok to contact this poster with services or other commercial interests

PostingID: 454851380

To: job-454851380@craigslist.org
Subject: Adult Volunteers needed for health tests
Date: Sat, 20 Oct 2007 22:24:36 EDT
From: ▇▇▇▇▇▇▇▇▇▇▇▇

hi

I have seen you ad regards to volunteer selection for experimental purpose. My question is for the first five weeks if you aren't going to provide food or experimental injection, then how will a volunteer survive? Please let me know.

I am interested in becoming your volunteer. I am a medical Science major and I graduated with BS degree in Cell Biology and anything involved with experiments facinates me. Please provide me with details of experiment location, and how much of compensation will you be paying me upfront and after experiment?

Looking forward to hear from you.

To: job-454851380@craigslist.org
Subject: Adult Volunteers needed for health tests
Date: Mon, 22 Oct 2007 05:18:06 -0700 (PDT)
From: ▇▇▇▇▇▇▇▇▇▇▇▇

Are you kidding me?!?!?!? Is this even ethical? What hospital would participate in something like this?

To: job-454851380@craigslist.org
Subject: Study
Date: Sat, 20 Oct 2007 18:37:06 -0400
From: ▇▇▇▇▇▇▇▇▇▇▇▇

I am interested! 27 year old healthy female... ▇▇▇▇▇

email this posting to a friend

please flag with care:
miscategorized
prohibited
spam/overpost
best of craigslist

Hunted seeking Bodyguard

Reply to: sale-454815127@craigslist.org
Date: 2007-10-20, 2:24PM PDT

I am a marked man. From Tulsa to Los Angeles, I have been followed by an ex convict. I am the only witness to a robbery he committed, and he wants me dead. The police were no help. Neither was witness protection. He's obsessed with finding me and killing me.

I need to hire a bodyguard. This position pays extremely well. Please hurry.

* it's NOT ok to contact this poster with services or other commercial interests

PostingID: 454815127

To: sale-454815127@craigslist.org
Subject: craigs list
Date: Sat, 20 Oct 2007 14:42:05 -0700 (PDT)
From: ███████████████

Well I can teach you how not be found, it will take some lifestyle adjustments but it can be done without a body guard.

cheers-

To: sale-454815127@craigslist.org
Subject: Hunted seeking Bodyguard
Date: Sat, 20 Oct 2007 20:26:32 EDT
From: ███████████████

How long do you need protection for and how much are you willing to pay? I have a partner I work with.

email this posting to a friend

please flag with care:
miscategorized
prohibited
spam/overpost
best of craigslist

I need a handyman to help me rebuild my neighbor's house

Reply to: serv-451390036@craigslist.org
Date: 2007-10-16, 9:32PM MST

My neighbors left me in charge of watering their plants and letting their dogs out while they went away to Minnesota for a week. They left on a Monday and by Wednesday, I'd lost both of their dogs and managed to plug up every toilet in the house. Then, on Thursday, I put some Jiffy Pop on the stove and fell asleep while watching Wayne's World. When I woke up, the kitchen was on fire.

Half of their house burned down before the firemen put the flames out. They're coming back in a week and I need to make it look like this never happened. We need to fix their house QUICK!

Please help me. And if you've seen two black labs running around, let me know.

* it's NOT ok to contact this poster with services or other commercial interests

PostingID: 451390036

To: serv-451390036@craigslist.org
Subject: I need a handyman to help me rebuild my neighbor's house
Date: Wed, 17 Oct 2007 02:10:45 -0700
From: ▊▊▊▊▊▊▊▊

Shut Up, No freakin' way nobody has that bad of luck except me. You have got to be kidding me. i have my own remodeling biz and would practily pay to see this and hear you tell the story face to face. ▊▊▊▊

▊▊▊▊▊▊▊▊▊▊

To: serv-451390036@craigslist.org
Subject: I need a handyman to help me rebuild my neighbor's house
Date: Wed, 17 Oct 2007 17:06:04 -0700
From: ▊▊▊▊▊▊▊▊

Wow, what a mess! I can come out and take a look if you are still needing

help out there. I can give you a quick written estimate and start work

immediately... Let me know!

Sorry, haven't seen the dogs!

Best Regards

▊▊▊▊

▊▊▊▊▊ Cell

▊▊▊▊▊ Fax

Hiring laborers to transport collection - $300

Reply to: job-xvysj-1084529712@craigslist.org
Date: 2009-03-20, 5:34PM PDT

I have a warehouse full of human skin and hair that needs to be transported across town, to the garment district, where the skin will be turned into suits and the hair will be turned into hats. Workers will be paid three hundred a day.

You will be offered discounts on skin suits and hair hats, as well as discounts on all the other fine products from my fashion line:

* Bone walking sticks
* Mustache eyebrows
* Skin leg warmers
* Fingernail sunglasses
* Tooth necklaces

* it's NOT ok to contact this poster with services or other commercial interests

PostingID: 1084529712

Sirs,

I can assist you I work daily for a local logistics company and have the moving/ delivery experience.

I am reached a ████████████

████████████████████

Wanted: Tattoo Artist for an idea I have - $4000

Reply to: sale-410296503@craigslist.org
Date: 2007-08-30, 6:51PM PDT

If you can draw my idea out Ill pay you well and even more if youll put it on my back (or stomach, you can decide which would look better)

This is what I want:

Jessica Rabbit from who framed roger rabbit is naked and riding a unicorn through a field. Next to her there's bamby who trots along smiling, but behind Bamby theres a baby Elmer Fudd in a diaper and he's pointing a rifle at Bamby. Theres a full moon overhead with the face of my grandmother, who passed six months ago god bless. Itll have her dates below in old English font. Then in the background theres a bunch of purple lightning and on top of a mountain theres a badass Honda RVF400 motorcycle just sitting there, looking over everything.

I'll give you six hundred just for the sketch, because I know its gonna be hard

* it's NOT ok to contact this poster with services or other commercial interests

PostingID: 410296503

To: sale-410296503@craigslist.org
Subject: Wanted: Tattoo Artist for an idea I have - $4000
Date: Thu, 6 Sep 2007 20:22:42 -0700 (PDT)
From: ███████████████

Hi My name is ██████. I'm interested in doing the artwork for You perhaps even the tattooing. You can check out My work on myspace if You like.

████████████████████████████

To: sale-410296503@craigslist.org
Subject: tat
Date: Thu, 6 Sep 2007 20:22:42 -0700 (PDT)
From: █████████████

i would like todo your tat. heres my web

████████████████████

i can sketch for you with down payment. ████████████

email this posting to a friend

please flag with care:
miscategorized
prohibited
spam/overpost
best of craigslist

Seeking daytime nanny

Reply to: comm-451362548@craigslist.org
Date: 2007-10-16, 8:50PM PDT

My husband and I are both very busy with work and can't stay at home to watch over our kids. We're looking to hire a daytime nanny to babysit, help around the house, maybe cook a meal every once in a while and clean on occasion. This position pays very well, because it won't be an easy job.

My son Jeremy is sixteen years old. He was expelled from high school for punching a teacher and is addicted to painkillers. Recently, he got a tattoo of Satan on his neck. He tortures small animals and rarely leaves his room. I don't know what to do with him.

My fifteen year old daughter Megan is pregnant. She smokes cigarettes, drinks beer, and is constantly sneaking guys into her room. We've tried everything to discipline her, but she's impossible.

My twelve year old son has severe autism.

Work would be Monday through Friday, eight AM to four PM.

* it's NOT ok to contact this poster with services or other commercial interests

PostingID: 451362548

To: comm-451362548@craigslist.org
Subject: Seeking daytime nanny
Date: Thu, 18 Oct 2007 15:40:59 -0700
From: ███████████

You need professional help. And I highly suggest a mediator. And most of all...your kids need GOD.
I am praying for you. I wish I could help. I'm praying for a way to help.

To: comm-451362548@craigslist.org
Subject: Seeking daytime nanny
Date: Thu, 18 Oct 2007 06:59:57 +0100 (BST)
From: ███████████

Hi my name is ██████. I am writing in reguards to your letter. Your family sounds a lot like mine. My older brother was the satan loving one and i was the teenage mother. I would love to be of assistance to you. I am a mother of 3. I have a 7 year old and Twins that are 3. I would love for you to give me the opportunity to get to know your wonderful children and to be of assistance to you. Thank you for you time and I hope to hear from you.You can contact me either by e-mail or by phone ███ ████████

Thank You, ███████████████████

To: comm-451362548@craigslist.org
Subject:
Date: Wed, 17 Oct 2007 15:05:18 GMT
From: ███████████

HI MY NAME IS ███████████ IM ██ YEARS OLD AND I HAVE EXSPERIENCE WORKING WITH KIDS WITH SPEACIAL NEEDS AND TROUBLE KIDS I JUST RECENTLY STOP WORKING FOR THE ARC OF SANDIEGO WHICH IS RESPECT CARE FOR FAMILYS WITH DISABILTY I KNOW EVERYTHING ABOUT AUSTIM I DONE ALOT BABYSITTING FOR THOS KIND OF KIDS IM CPR AND FIRST AIDE TRAIN IM A CHRISTIAN I DONT DRINK OR SMOKE OR DO DRUGS I HAVE OVER 30 YEARS EXSPEREINCE WORKING WITH KIDS AND INFIANTS

████████

PS I HAVE CPR CERTIFICATE AND BEEN FINGER PRINTED THROUGH TRUSTLINE AND LIVESCAN

[42 | Wanted: Bear Cubs for My Children]

email this posting to a friend

Wanted: Author for already-sold children's book

Reply to: gigs-416009814@craigslist.org
Date: 2007-09-07, 12:15AM EDT

My husband is a well respected literary agent here in Manhattan and I recently sold him on an idea for a children's book, which he then sold to a large publishing house (which shall remain undisclosed until we're in further talks). I am in need of a writer to make my idea come to life. It's something I've been thinking about since I was a kid and I've waited to unveil it until the time was right. Well, the time is now.

The book is titled "Snoopy Goes Poopy" and its all about Snoopy the dog teaching children how to use the bathroom. In it, Snoopy shows children how to go number 2. The Peanuts gang also assure children that it is perfectly normal to go poopy, and that yes, even Snoopy goes poopy. I've fleshed out a preliminary page outline, which reads as follows:

  Page 1: Snoopy is on top of his doghouse sleeping. He then gets an ache in his stomach and knows that he must use the lawn as a bathroom.
  Page 2: Snoopy goes poopy.
  Page 3: The Peanuts gang notice Snoopy going number 2 and they assure child readers that this is perfectly normal, and that yes, even Charley Brown goes to the bathroom this way.
  Page 4: Instructions on how to properly "go poopy"

This may seem like a silly idea, but I think it has a massive marketing potential. It is also, for the prospective writer, a very lucrative project. Please reply with credentials and samples.

* it's NOT ok to contact this poster with services or other commercial interests

PostingID: 416009814

To: gigs-416009814@craigslist.org
Subject: Wanted: Author for already-sold children's book
Date: Fri, 7 Sep 2007 17:37:14 -0100
From: ███████████████

What in the world would possess you to think you could steal copyrighted characters and adapt them for you dumbass poopy doopy campaign? I cannot believe the crazies out there like you on CL. You should run for president of the CL Nutty Buddy Society!!!

To: gigs-416009814@craigslist.org
Subject: wait a second
Date: Fri, 7 Sep 2007 07:41:49 EDT
From: ███████████████

snoopy doesnt speak. that is the only problem. It sounds do-able....I think, except it is a little strange because you got the kids checking him out as he drops the deuce. I am laughing, but it is because I am a child at heart, hopefully. I am a freelance writer, collaborating with ███████████ for scripts right now. My brother loves snoopy, that is why I am writing to you. I can not send you anything over email, because it is not copyrighted. However if you did want to go further, we could go back and fourth with ideas, and try it that way?? I can be reached best by reply to this email. Thank you for your time. Bye.

Publisher seeking slash writers for new slash anthology

Reply to: gigs-419032634@craigslist.org
Date: 2007-09-10, 5:35PM EDT

I work for a prominent publisher that deals mostly in gay lit. We're looking to publish an anthology of slash. We've already gotten several hundred submissions. From the looks of it, we have enough Harry Potter, GI Joe, Pokemon, Final Fantasy 7 and Drew Carey Show fiction. What we are looking to do is hire slash writers to develop the following pairings into short stories:

1.) Magneto (XMen) / Archie (from the Archie Comics)
2.) Bill O'Reilly / Karl Rove
3.) Elton John / Eminem
4.) Dagwood (from the Blondie Comics) / Dilbert
5.) Spiderman / Leisure Suit Larry
6.) Linkin Park / Fat Albert and his band
7.) Homer Simpson / Larry the Cable Guy
8.) Dad from the Family Circus / Andy Dick

AND ANY OTHER PAIRINGS YOU CAN THINK OF! Submit samples alongside pitches. Thanks!

* it's NOT ok to contact this poster with services or other commercial interests

PostingID: 419032634

To: gigs-419032634@craigslist.org
Subject: Publisher seeking slash writers for new slash anthology
Date: Tue, 11 Sep 2007 01:56:46 -0700 (PDT)
From: ████████████████

Dear editor/publisher,

Considering some of your pairings, I'm not sure if this is a serious post, but if it is, I would be interested in submitting something. I have a Speed Racer/Racer X slash that is about 75% finished (it's not humorous but more like 'literary erotica"). If this is something that you would be interested in seeing, let me know. Do you have guidelines? What are your word count min/max and pay rate?

I am a published writer and editor (horror, sci-fi, fantasy) and am also into yaoi (I attended YaoiCon in San Francisco the past two years)

See links below for more on me.

I look forward to hearing back from you.

Best wishes,

████████

██████████████████

█████████████████

Wanted: Tattoo Artist to Sketch My Idea - $1000

Reply to: sale-409518298@craigslist.org
Date: 2007-08-29, 10:34PM CDT

Let me say I'll pay you well if you can draw this out and then put it on my back (I have several thousand). It's gonna sound silly but I've been thinking about this fer a really long time and I need to get it done before I join the Marines.

Heres my idea:

Theres a carebear in a monster truck (the popular blue one) driving over a skeleton on a flaming motorcycle with a naked woman on the back. Behind them He-Man and the Masters of the Universe are fighting with some bad guys and there's a Mount Rushmore with all the basketball players they did on "Mount Dunkmore" (I think it was Jordan, Pippin, Barkely and David Robinson) back in the 90s. Then, on top of Mount Dunkmore, I'm wearing a Bulls starter jacket and holding a sword to the sky. Its He-Man's sword.

The reason I want all of this on my back is because they're all my favorite things.

* it's NOT ok to contact this poster with services or other commercial interests

PostingID: 409518298

To: sale-409518298@craigslist.org
Subject: Wanted: Tattoo Artist to Sketch My Idea - $1000
Date: Fri, 31 Aug 2007 18:49:22 -0500
From: ▓▓▓▓▓▓▓▓▓▓▓▓▓

no problem - sounds like a good idea - come into ▓▓▓▓▓▓▓▓▓▓▓▓▓▓▓▓▓▓ to
set up your appoinment - will require a deposit though to get started on the drawing
- $500 down

▓▓▓▓

▓▓▓▓▓▓▓▓▓▓

▓▓▓▓▓▓▓

▓▓▓▓▓▓▓

To: sale-409518298@craigslist.org
Subject: Wanted: Tattoo Artist to Sketch My Idea - $1000
Date: Tue, 4 Sep 2007 15:25:18 -0500
From: ▓▓▓▓▓▓▓▓▓▓▓

Please send me a picture of this when you get it drawn up. That is the best tattoo
idea ever!!!!!!

Need a couple of guys to kick my roommate's ass

Reply to: sale-505484677@craigslist.org
Date: 2007-12-11, 12:02AM EST

My roommate is a total fucking dick. He moved here from out of town six months ago, answered my "roommate wanted" ad, took over my second bedroom, and has yet to pay me rent or a deposit. All day, he sits around in his robe watching soap operas and eating cereal, smoking two packs a day INSIDE, despite our building's strict "No Smoking" policy. I've caught him having sex on my couch SIX TIMES with nasty bar skanks. He drinks all of my beer and scratches all of my DVDs. He refuses to get a job and blows all his parent's money on weed. On top of that, he's stolen AT LEAST four hundred dollars from me and caused my girlfriend to move out.

This guy needs to get his ass kicked. Bad. I ask him every day to move out, and every day I come home from work and he hasn't left the couch. The thing is, he's bigger than me. And the one time I tried to hit him, he put me in a head lock and then threw me through a glass table.

If you're willing to come over and kick my roommate's ass, I'll make it worth your while.

* it's NOT ok to contact this poster with services or other commercial interests

PostingID: 505484677

To: sale-505484677@craigslist.org
Date: Tue, 11 Dec 2007 06:47:11 EST
Subject: Need a couple of guys to kick my roommate's ass
From: ███████████████

please contact me asap about fucking up your roommate

To: sale-505484677@craigslist.org
Subject: Need a couple of guys to kick my roommate's ass
Date: Tue, 11 Dec 2007 06:47:11 EST
From: ███████████████

I will be happy to do so, where are you located?

To: sale-505484677@craigslist.org
Subject: Need a couple of guys to kick my roommate's ass
Date: Tue, 11 Dec 2007 06:47:11 EST
From: ███████████████

this guy sounds like a real douche bag.......how big is this guy and how old is he......
i dont need to get in trouble if hes not at least 18 im 6'4" 300lbs and can hold my
own....i dont think he has the balls to try and put me in a headlock......so what
compensation are we talking about?

Chapter 3: Sexual Advances

A glossary of terms you'll encounter in the following pages:

m4m: Male for Male.

w4m: Woman for Male.

NSA: No Strings Attached—sex with a stranger.

Bottom: The partner in a sexual encounter that receives.

Cut: Circumcised.

Bi: Bisexual.

DDF: Drug and Disease Free.

Furry: One who gets pleasure from dressing up as an animal.

Dominatrix: A female who is the dominant partner in a sadomasochistic sexual encounter.

Looner: One who fetishizes balloons.

Hard Crush: The act of crushing things under one's foot for the pleasure of others.

Zookeeper wanting NSA - w4m

Reply to: pers-421047117@craigslist.org
Date: 2007-09-12, 9:26AM CDT

I work at the zoo as a feeder and becuase of that I got the keys. Im in charge of soome of the bigger animals and all day im thinking about breaking into the cages and getting it on in there while the lions are sleeping. for some reason I cant get this idea out of my head its been haunting me for two years now so I have to do it. I want you to come with me into the zoo and it would have to be late (maybe two AM or three). Ill give the lions a sedative to make them sleep for a little while and we will go from there, im thinking in this nice fake waterfall area by where they feed.

Im a single white female, in shape and have only had a few boyfriends so I don't have any problems ore diseases or anything like that. You need to be very quiet for all of this and you need to be clean and in pretty good shape.

* it's NOT ok to contact this poster with services or other commercial interests

PostingID: 421047117

To: pers-421047117@craigslist.org
Subject: Zookeeper wanting NSA - w4m
Date: Wed, 12 Sep 2007 22:45:13 EDT
From: ███████████

wow, Having sex in a cage with lions or coyotes /wolves has also been a fantasy of
mine. I would love to try that with you. And if they wake up oh well and we can what
may happen than????? I would really like to try that, pleas write me back

---

To: pers-421047117@craigslist.org
Subject: Zookeeper wanting NSA - w4m
Date: Wed, 12 Sep 2007 21:46:07 EDT
From: ███████████

You have a very cool and fun idea.

We can be animals in their environment.

We should bring a camera for future reference.

Hope you like me . . . cause I know you probably got a lot of

   responses.

███████████

To: pers-421047117@craigslist.org
Subject: re:craigslist
Date: Wed, 12 Sep 2007 19:52:35 (PDT)
From: ███████████

hi i think your idea is increadible...i've never ever thought about something like
that but it sounds great. message me back and we'll find a way to get in touch if
interested in me

To: pers-421047117@craigslist.org
Subject: Seriously?
Date: Wed, 12 Sep 2007 19:52:35 (PDT)
From: ████████████████

Alright, your ad caught my eye and I will admit you have me intrigued. When are you looking to do this, and isnt there security at the zoo during the night? I am clean, d/d free, and I am in good enough shape to run from waking lions ;)

If this is where I am thinking it is, that would be really cool. Tell me more of what you've got in mind.

████████

email this posting to a friend

please flag with care:
miscategorized
prohibited
spam/overpost
best of craigslist

Drive over me with your car - w4m

Reply to: pers-qp68e-1084541237@craigslist.org
Date: 2009-03-20, 5:43PM PDT

This sort of thing really gets me off.

* it's NOT ok to contact this poster with services or other commercial interests

PostingID: 1084541237

To: pers-qp68e-1084541237@craigslist.org
Subject: ol
Date: Sat, 21 Mar 2009 1:28 AM
From: ███████████

Lets do it

To: pers-qp68e-1084541237@craigslist.org
Subject: your ad..
Date: Sat, 21 Mar 2009 1:18 AM
From: ███████████

i have a truck, will that work?

To: pers-qp68e-1084541237@craigslist.org
Subject: Drive over me with your car - w4m
Date: Sat, 21 Mar 2009 1:20 AM
From: ███████████

I am free right know and have

time too spend if you want this too happen

email this posting to a friend

please flag with care:
miscategorized
prohibited
spam/overpost
best of craigslist

Methodist minister seeking bottom - m4m - 41

Reply to: pers-419041786@craigslist.org
Date: 2007-09-10, 4:45PM CDT

I'm looking for a bottom for next Tuesday or Wednesday, when my family is out of town. I'm a minister in town and this needs to be completely discreet. I will not pay you, but I will show you a very good time. No fatties.

* it's NOT ok to contact this poster with services or other commercial interests

PostingID: 419041786

To: pers-419041786@craigslist.org
Subject: your CL ad
Date: Mon, 10 Sep 2007 15:04:10 -0700 (PDT)
From: ███████████████

I'm also a clergyman, so I need ultra discreet situations. I'm 46, bisexual 5'9" 165 32w 6' cut, bi white. Cannot host. I prefer other bi men, but I'm not averse to getting it on with a gay man, as long as we are always safe. I am H/W proportionate, but not in good shape, a situation I have started to remedy at the beginning of September.

please let me know of your interest ASAP. I do not send face pix and can only meet tomorrow night not Wednesday.

To: pers-419041786@craigslist.org
Subject: may i
Date: Mon, 10 Sep 2007 15:41:31 -0700 (PDT)
From: ███████████████

kneel before you to receive, and drink deeply.

very very serious here. bimwm here so discreet

and ddf is required. i am very talented at helping

a guy achieve powerful multiple orgasms.

To: pers-419041786@craigslist.org
Subject: Methodist minister seeking bottom - 41
Date: Tue, 11 Sep 2007 10:52:21 EDT
From: ███████████████

I'm a builder with a private suburban house. Garage for the car, total discretion and fun.

please flag with care:
miscategorized
prohibited
spam/overpost
best of craigslist

Fulfill my fantasy, boys - w4m

Reply to: pers-419028699@craigslist.org
Date: 2007-09-10, 5:31PM EDT

I'm a 21 year old college student, a bit overweight but still pretty and sexy. I have had this fantasy for three years and I want to do it with someone. Here's what I have in mind:

I will dress up like Roseanne Barr from the television show Roseanne and you will dress up like Dan (John Goodman). We will then act out a scene from the show, and in the middle of the scene, make love on the dinner table (even though it is already set with a meal).

Please make this come true for me.

* it's NOT ok to contact this poster with services or other commercial interests

PostingID: 419028699

To: pers-419028699@craigslist.org
Subject: Fulfill my fantasy, boys - w4m
Date: Mon, 10 Sep 2007 16:29:09 -0700 (PDT)
From: ████████████████

I think i remember seeign them do that in an episode that would be so fun!!

Hi, there is no way i could not respond to your ad. Ia m30 yrs old near lauderdale.
You honestly sound interesting..i would like to know u are for real before we get to
talking , ask me anything you want to know i will answer honestly. Email me back
so i know you are for real. I dont think the women on here realize how many ads are
not real ppl, this is why i send my pic after a response. hope you understand that. As
soon as you email me back i will send pics before i ask for yours. like i said anything
you would like to know just ask. get back soon no sense in wasting the rest of the
night:)

To: pers-419028699@craigslist.org
Subject: hi
Date: Mon, 10 Sep 2007 18:11:47 -0400 (EDT)
From: ████████████████

hello maybe but the time u get my e mail u problaly had recive like 100

but I give u a try

me 511 190lb

i like to see you and that would be a first to me but sounds interesting

hey if my e mail got u atention great hope i hear from u

later ████████

To: pers-419028699@craigslist.org
Subject: how can i help
Date: Mon, 10 Sep 2007 16:29:09 -0700 (PDT)
From: ████████████████

25/m here

please flag with care:
miscategorized
prohibited
spam/overpost
best of craigslist

Pee on me - w4m - 26

Reply to: pers-399653478@craigslist.org
Date: 2007-08-17, 8:35AM EDT

Oh, will you please pee on me?

* it's NOT ok to contact this poster with services or other commercial interests

PostingID: 399653478

To: pers-399653478@craigslist.org
Subject: Pee on me - w4m - 26
Date: Fri, 17 Aug 2007 21:32:11 EDT
From: ███████████████
CC: ███████████████

Sure.

To: pers-399653478@craigslist.org
Subject: pee on me
Date: Fri, 17 Aug 2007 17:53:33 -0700 (PDT)
From: ███████████████

hello

lets get together and let me pee on u.............

To: pers-399653478@craigslist.org
Subject: Pee on me - w4m - 26
Date: Fri, 17 Aug 2007 20:55:03 EDT
From: ███████████████

if u come to me, i'll pee on you, i'm in queens

To: pers-399653478@craigslist.org
Subject: C-c-c-craigslist.........
Date: Fri, 17 Aug 2007 20:44:49 -0400
From: ███████████████

I cant beleive you're serious but I'm really into this sorta thing, as strange as it may seem. I"m at home in williamsburg watching the food network and bored as can be I have a car and can come pick you up if you'd likkkkkkkkkkeeeee....

AIM?!?!

MYSPACE?!?!

Your thoughts on Woody Allen!??!?

email this posting to a friend

please flag with care:
miscategorized
prohibited
spam/overpost
best of craigslist

Middle Aged Woman Seeking NSA with a Christmas Tree - w4m

Reply to: pers-455792831@craigslist.org
Date: 2007-10-21, 9:33PM EDT

My husband of twenty five years left me six months ago for his secretary. Since then, I've been without sex and very lonely. We share joint custody of our children and I have a lot of free time on my hands. I've been thinking a lot about what would fulfill my fantasies, and decided that I want to sleep with a man dressed up as a Christmas tree.

Christmas has always been my favorite holiday. I wait eleven months out of the year for December to roll around, and when it does, I spend every day decorating my house, wrapping gifts, and listening to carols. I dream at night about Santa Claus and gingerbread men. I love everything about Christmas. I love the look on my children's faces as they unwrap presents. I love wearing snowman sweaters and Rudolph earrings. But most of all, I love the Christmas tree. I love sitting in the dark, with the tree's lights reflecting off its tinsel, drinking eggnog and singing "Santa Claus is coming to town." I love the smell of the needles. I love topping it with a white angel. And I love, love, love putting ornaments on it.

I need you to dress up like a Christmas tree and have sex with me.

* it's NOT ok to contact this poster with services or other commercial interests

PostingID: 455792831

To: pers-455792831@craigslist.org
Subject: Middle Aged Woman Seeking NSA with a Christmas Tree - w4m
Date: Sun, 21 Oct 2007 21:57:45 -0400
From: ████████████

lady u have got to be out of your freaking mind

To: pers-455792831@craigslist.org
Subject: Middle Aged Woman Seeking NSA with a Christmas Tree - w4m
Date: Sun, 21 Oct 2007 19:15:56 -0700 (PDT)
From: ████████████████

I suppose I could dress up as a xmas tree babe, where town are you located in? can you send me a pic? I am 50something, white, clean and fit. interested hun?

To: pers-455792831@craigslist.org
Date: Mon, 22 Oct 2007 11:41:16 -0700 (PDT)
Subject: Do you have a christmas tree outfit?
From: ████████████████

Do you own a christmas tree outfit? Can you rent one or do you have to buy something like that. This may be one of the weirdest things i've ever read but i'm still intregued. I'm a younger man and may be interested. I'm 20 years old. If you have a picture that would be nice. I send mine when i see yours. Thanks

████████

To: pers-455792831@craigslist.org
Subject: Middle Aged Woman Seeking NSA with a Christmas Tree - w4m
Date: Mon, 22 Oct 2007 04:55:12 -0700 (PDT)
From: ████████████████

how sound very nice an intresting but where would you find a christmas tree outfit ?? i would do it in a heart beat am 6 ft 1 so a big tree would be in bed with you . i usuaal dree up as santa for our union kids party . am in law enforcement   let me know thanks ██████

[64 | Wanted: Bear Cubs for My Children]

email this posting to a friend

please flag with care:
miscategorized
prohibited
spam/overpost
best of craigslist

24f seeking NSA Fantasy - w4m

Reply to: pers-421053635@craigslist.org
Date: 2007-09-12, 10:35PM EDT

I'm looking for a portly man to fulfill my ultimate fantasy. As a child, I was swarmed in the park by squirrels and fell to the ground. The squirrels bit into my clothing and broke my skin. It was the first time I felt an erotic sensation, and I'm looking to recreate it.

I've purchased a squirrel mascot from a nearby costume shop. I want you to wear it.

* it's NOT ok to contact this poster with services or other commercial interests

PostingID: 421053635

To: pers-421053635@craigslist.org
Subject: fucked by a squirrel
Date: Thu, 13 Sep 2007 07:54:23 -0700
From: ██████████████

I'll do it. I'm not crazy and I don't think you are too. But I think thinnk it would be a good ice breaker. Heck you may just want to keep doing it once in a while. I could cut a little hole in the costume so you can have sex with the costume on.

To: pers-421053635@craigslist.org
Subject: 24f seeking NSA Fantasy - w4m
Date: Fri, 14 Sep 2007 00:01:55 -0400
From: ██████████████

Ok, I'll play along, but on a tit for tat basis. If I fulfill your fantasy, I would need you to fulfill mine. I need to pretend that you are a naughty school girl, and you get sent to my office for not wearing panties to school that day. As the Dean, I'm obligated to call your parents, but you're willing to do anything to keep that from happening. Let me know if that interests you.

To: pers-421053635@craigslist.org
Subject: Criags List
Date: Wed, 12 Sep 2007 19:47:18 -0700 (PDT)
From: ██████████████

I'm game. Honey I will wear what you want and bite you wherever you like.

To: pers-421053635@craigslist.org
Subject: 24f seeking NSA Fantasy - w4m
Date: Wed, 12 Sep 2007 19:52:30 -0700 (PDT)
From: ██████████████

I'm interested. Just email me a pic of yourself and the costume. I might be able to do it friday morning around 11:00am. I'm a little overweight.

I'm looking to pick up some STD's - w4m

Reply to: pers-455773027@craigslist.org
Date: 2007-10-21, 9:07PM EDT

My ex-boyfriend of eight years cheated on me a month ago with my best friend and moved out. Two nights ago, he came by my place drunk and we had sex. We're supposed to meet up again on Tuesday. I would like to contract some STDs before then.

If you're looking to have a no-strings-attached experience with a 26 year old, athletic brunette, and you have an STD, please contact me.

* it's NOT ok to contact this poster with services or other commercial interests

PostingID: 455773027

To: pers-455773027@craigslist.org
Subject: I'm looking to pick up some STD's - w4m
Date: Sun, 21 Oct 2007 21:18:26 EDT
From: ███████████

45 white male with stds if interested e-mail me

To: pers-455773027@craigslist.org
Subject: I'm looking to pick up some STD's - w4m
Date: Mon, 22 Oct 2007 01:06:00 EDT
From: ███████████

ARE YOU FUCKING
CRAZY??/

To: pers-455773027@craigslist.org
Subject: I'm looking to pick up some STD's - w4m
Date: Sun, 21 Oct 2007 21:28:26 EDT
From: ███████████

ummm why would u do that thats fuked up n even if he hert u witch i get dont do that to urself u dont want a std just do sumtin n let him find out insted or sumtin fuk sum guy on tape n let him find it or play it on axadent or sumshit dont do that to urself im sure ur an amazin woman who can get alout n do alout in her life i know it hurts my gf cheated on mme but thats not th4 way to go

---

To: pers-455773027@craigslist.org
Subject: I'm looking to pick up some STD's - w4m
Date: Sun, 21 Oct 2007 19:39:24 -0700 (PDT)
From: ███████████

how would u like to make it burn when he pees....I can help....I can give you free antibiotics too if you want....

Furry M 22 (Unicorn) - m4m - 22

Reply to: pers-396423317@craigslist.org
Date: 2007-08-13, 7:02PM PDT

Hey there!

I'm a cute little unicorn and i'm looking for another fur to come along and sweep me off my hooves :) I like wolves and bears but am open for jus about anything! Could be just a casual yiff or some scritching, whatever you think sounds fun. i'm just a fun little guy and I'm new to the area. Don't know any other furs and I'm dying to get myself out there!

Reply with pics if you got um but if not lets just talk, ok? I won't bite! (or maybe I will...:)

* it's NOT ok to contact this poster with services or other commercial interests

PostingID: 396423317

To: pers-396423317@craigslist.org
Subject: Unicorn
Date: Mon, 13 Aug 2007 20:22:32 (GMT-07:00)
From: ███████████████

I have a butterfly and a rat (terrier) and fur

and a horn

nice post

I'm 34

To: pers-396423317@craigslist.org
Subject: Furry M 22 (Unicorn) - m4m - 22
Date: Mon, 13 Aug 2007 20:28:56 -07:00
From: ███████████████

hey man, i'll be ur unicorn. :-) him me back.

████████████

email this posting to a friend

please flag with care:
miscategorized
prohibited
spam/overpost
best of craigslist

Hottie seeking - 27

Reply to: pers-417386018@craigslist.org
Date: 2007-09-08, 4:49PM EDT

Hello. My name is Amanda. I'm 27, 5'6, 140 pounds, and muscular. I am looking for a manly guy to take me out. I am a Klanswoman and am looking for a lifelong Klansman to date. Potential dates must be Klan, no exceptions, and must have a nice body and short hair.

For fun, I like going to movies and dining out, as well as seeing concerts and cooking. If you are into any of these things, a Klansman, and in good shape, please reply (and pics would be nice, too!)

* it's NOT ok to contact this poster with services or other commercial interests

PostingID: 417386018

To: pers-417386018@craigslist.org
Subject: The Klan?
Date: Sun, 9 Sep 2007 11:24:43 -0700 (PDT)
From: ███████████████

Hello Amanda,

I am writing in regards to your advertisement on Craigslist. I am not in the Klan, though I have connections to the Klan in MS and could very easily become one if so desired.

If you are interested let me know and i'll send pics and/or contact info.

Takecare...Later.

To: pers-417386018@craigslist.org
Subject:
Date: Mon, 10 Sep 2007 00:29:35 -0400
From: ▮▮▮▮▮▮▮▮▮▮

hi im ▮▮▮▮ im just like the klan though im not in but,would like to be in

sosososo bad hell yea that rocks that u like klan men

go KKK babe

im kinda new to here

been here for 7 months now

well,im 6 foot 2 incheds tall

180lbs.

22 years old

well,here is my picture let me know if

ur interested

hope to hear from u seen

▮▮▮▮▮

To: pers-417386018@craigslist.org
Subject: Hey
Date: Fri, 14 Sep 2007 08:01:03 -0400
From: ▮▮▮▮▮▮▮▮▮▮

BURN IN HELL YOU COWARD ASS BITCH! FUCKING KLANSMEN ARE
BITCHES. COME OUT IN REAL LIFE AND TALK YOUR CRAP!

I'M NOT RACIST AND I LOVE MY WHITE MAN. I JUST HATE RACIST PEOPLE!

email this posting to a friend

please flag with care:
miscategorized
prohibited
spam/overpost
best of craigslist

Light my house on fire - w4m

Reply to: pers-25mwc-1084548222@craigslist.org
Date: 2009-03-20, 5:49PM PDT

This sort of thing really gets me off.

* it's NOT ok to contact this poster with services or other commercial interests

PostingID: 1084548222

To: pers-25mwc-1084548222@craigslist.org
Subject: [No Subject]
Date: Sat, 21 Mar 2009 1:19 AM
From: ▆▆▆▆▆▆▆▆▆▆

well il give a ride you wont for get

email this posting to a friend

please flag with care:
miscategorized
prohibited
spam/overpost
best of craigslist

Dominatrix Seeking Slaves - w4m - 27

Reply to: pers-396470917@craigslist.org
Date: 2007-08-13, 8:01PM PDT

I'm a chubby white Dominatrix with a full bondage basement looking to meet up with a slave. I wear full leather when the kids aren't around and I'm a bad little lady, you better believe it. I used to charge for it but now I just wanna have some fun.

You: wanting to be pushed around and hurt to the point of ecstasy.

Me: wanting to push you around and hurt you to the point of ecstasy.

I love pain and you should too. Reply with pics.

* it's NOT ok to contact this poster with services or other commercial interests

PostingID: 396470917

To: pers-396470917@craigslist.org
Subject: Your posting looking for extreme pain slaves
Date: Wed, 15 Aug 2007 23:18:29 -0700 (PDT)
From: ████████████████████

Dearest Mistress-

This is in response to Your recent posting looking for pain slaves. Has the position already been filled? This lowly one has an very high pain threshold (correction: low threshold that can be stretched extremely far if You are receiving pleasure from my agony). It should be an honor to suffer for You. i am on the road right now and do not have a photo, but if You can please send me You e-mail address i shall send You one when i return.

At Your feet, in tears always,

████████

To: pers-396470917@craigslist.org
Subject: Hello Mistress
Date: Mon, 13 Aug 2007 20:20:25 -0700 (PDT)
From: ████████████████████

Mistress- permission to ask a few questions?

To: pers-396470917@craigslist.org
Subject: re: Dominatrix Seeking Slaves
Date: Fri, 17 Aug 2007 18:02:57 -0700 (PDT)
From: ████████████████████

on my knees, looking up at Your leather clad form, breath coming slowly ,heart racing in anticipation of enduring and feeling the inf;iction of Your pain.................

email this posting to a friend

please flag with care:
miscategorized
prohibited
spam/overpost
best of craigslist

Balloon fetishist looking for looner partner - m4m - 31

Reply to: pers-419052666@craigslist.org
Date: 2007-09-10, 5:57PM EDT

Loony looking to have fun with balloons! If you're a looner and you want to get together some time soon, please please please reply to this ad! I need you!

* it's NOT ok to contact this poster with services or other commercial interests

PostingID: 419052666

To: pers-419052666@craigslist.org
Subject: Balloon fetishist looking for looner partner - m4m - 31
Date: Mon, 10 Sep 2007 18:56:25 EDT
From: ███████████████

Hi there: I am intrigued.   Just how loony do you want???

Make a sandwich out of me - w4m

Reply to: pers-vhx9b-1085635859@craigslist.org
Date: 2009-03-21, 1:13PM MST

Last week, a baker friend made me two seven-foot-tall slices of white bread. Yesterday at CostCo I purchased twelve heads of lettuce, thirty tomatoes, ten jars of mustard, and sixteen pounds of Muenster cheese. Everything is prepped and ready to go. I want you to make a giant sandwich of me.

I'll lay atop one of the bread slices. You'll slather me with mustard, shower me with lettuce and tomatoes and cheese, and put the other slice over me.

It will be delicious.

* it's NOT ok to contact this poster with services or other commercial interests

PostingID: 1085635859

To: pers-vhx9b-1085635859@craigslist.org
Subject: Make a sandwich out of me - w4m
Date: Sat, 21 Mar 2009 8:53 PM
From: ▮▮▮▮▮▮▮▮▮▮▮▮

We can make that happen, hit me up asap

To: pers-vhx9b-1085635859@craigslist.org
Subject: sandwhich for lunch
Date: Sat, 21 Mar 2009 8:33 PM
From: ▮▮▮▮▮▮▮▮▮▮▮

i would like to come over for lunch and make you into the sexiest sandwhich ever. i
am white 26 have pics and am 100% real

email this posting to a friend

please flag with care:
miscategorized
prohibited
spam/overpost
best of craigslist

Hard Crush Fetishist Seeking Partner - w4m - 27

Reply to: pers-419049191@craigslist.org
Date: 2007-09-10, 2:53PM PDT

Seeking a partner to stomp things in front of me. I have candies, toys, mice, lizards and cigars. In return, I will put on my red stilettos and crush whatever you'd like.

Masturbation is optional.

* it's NOT ok to contact this poster with services or other commercial interests

PostingID: 419049191

To: pers-419049191@craigslist.org
Subject: Hard Crush Fetishist Seeking Partner - w4m - 27
Date: Mon, 10 Sep 2007 16:00:07 -0700
From: ███████████████

You turn me on, Let's get crushing! ██████

To: pers-419049191@craigslist.org
Subject: lets stomp away.
Date: Mon, 10 Sep 2007 16:25:24 -0700
From: ███████████████

What do you want me to wear when I stomp? What will turn you on and make you masturbate?

To: pers-419049191@craigslist.org
Subject: Hard Crush Fetishist Seeking Partner - w4m - 27
Date: Mon, 10 Sep 2007 18:08:54 EDT
From: ███████████████

WHAT IF ID LIKE YOU TO MASTURBATE ME?

email this posting to a friend

please flag with care:
miscategorized
prohibited
spam/overpost
best of craigslist

Crazy girl looking for insane night out - w4m

Reply to: pers-tkveb-1084537731@craigslist.org
Date: 2009-03-20, 8:55PM EDT

Here's what I want to do tonight:

Sniff glue * Smoke glue * Drink a bottle of rubbing alcohol * Paint the sidewalk with cattle blood * Smoke cattle blood * Roll around in a campfire * Drive my car into a storefront * Walk backwards across interstate traffic in a blindfold * Lick the roof of your mouth * Punch a stop sign *

INTERESTED?

* it's NOT ok to contact this poster with services or other commercial interests

PostingID: 1084537731

To: pers-tkveb-1084537731@craigslist.org
Subject: Crazy girl looking for insane night out - w4m
Date: Sat, 21 Mar 2009 2:14 AM
From: ██████████████

thats all what will we do after that ? age ? pic where in bk r u . so you had a week like mine i take it

---

To: pers-tkveb-1084537731@craigslist.org
Subject: Planters?
Date: Sat, 21 Mar 2009 1:12 AM
From: ██████████████

You sound like a nut!

email this posting to a friend

please flag with care:
miscategorized
prohibited
spam/overpost
best of craigslist

Please guys make this happen for me - w4m

Reply to: pers-421057986@craigslist.org
Date: 2007-09-12, 7:42PM PDT

Ive had this fantasy for a really long time and I need it to come true because its all I can think about sometimes. I was an exhibitionist when I was in college but Ive toned it down the past five years since I started my career but I have an idea. I really really really want to break into someones house and sneak into their living room. There, we will have it on the couch, very quietly. I am not kidding, please pplease please make this happen for me.

* it's NOT ok to contact this poster with services or other commercial interests

PostingID: 421057986

To: pers-421057986@craigslist.org
Subject: i'm down
Date: Wed, 12 Sep 2007 20:14:45 -0700 (PDT)
From: ████████

you better be really hot and know what youre doing

To: pers-421057986@craigslist.org
Subject: Please guys make this happen for me - w4m
Date: Thu, 13 Sep 2007 03:52:55 EDT
From: ████████

if you are on line tonight let me know asap... im down for this and able.. im 5'8" and

160.. very athletic build.. green eyea and good looking.. also a fast runner lol..

To: pers-421057986@craigslist.org
Subject: Please guys make this happen for me - w4m
Date: Wed, 12 Sep 2007 22:56:34 -0700 (PDT)
From: ████████

im down,when r you planning to do this?

Chapter 4: Dating

Is there anything more depressing than the online dating scene? You're probably saying to yourself: Yes, of course, I can think of five or six things that are more depressing than the online dating scene. Foreign war. Poverty. Famine. Disease. School shootings. Daytime television.

But trust me, after doing this little "experiment," I can tell you: online dating is up there with famine.

email this posting to a friend

please flag with care:
miscategorized
prohibited
spam/overpost
best of craigslist

Take me and my baby skydiving

Reply to: pers-451375842@craigslist.org
Date: 2007-10-16, 11:09PM CDT

I'm looking for a man to take me and my six month old Tanya skydiving. I'm a single mother, 22 years old, used to be a cheerleader but now I'm a fitness trainer. I always wanted to take my baby skydiving because she used to love it when her daddy did the "airplane" and held her over his head. Well, he died three months ago, so I'm looking for a new relationship.

After the skydive, we could go to a nice Italian restaurant and have some wine. I'm a real nice woman and a good lover. The road to my heart is paved with you taking me and my baby skydiving. You won't regret it.

* it's NOT ok to contact this poster with services or other commercial interests

PostingID: 451375842

To: pers-451375842@craigslist.org
Subject: craigs listing - in case
Date: Wed, 17 Oct 2007 18:15:20 -0700 (PDT)
From: ███████████████

in case you are not joking, and are stupid enough to do it, do not take your baby skydiving hahahhahahah sorry too funny.

no one is that retarded...

....

....

or are they?

To: pers-451375842@craigslist.org
Subject: C/L Post
Date: Tue, 16 Oct 2007 21:30:41 -0700 (PDT)
From: ███████████████

You want to have your baby jump out of an airplane? Are you crazy? Or, am I missing something here?

To: pers-451375842@craigslist.org
Subject: Take me and my baby skydiving
Date: Tue, 16 Oct 2007 21:38:10 -0700 (PDT)
From: ███████████████

I would love to take you sky-diving. I have never gone, but I am always open to try it.

███████

email this posting to a friend

Looking for love - 31

Reply to: pers-419018480@craigslist.org
Date: 2007-09-10, 2:20PM PDT

My name is Mary. I haven't left my apartment in four years. I have twenty two cats and a collection of dolls that keep me company, but they've been making teams and lying to me and I need to be with a real human but I can't face the idea of leaving my apartment and facing the people on the streets. The cats have broken into four families and they have built their own houses out of cardboard and Styrofoam. The families have begun quarreling and I can't stand the sound of their arguments. The dolls have built an impressive castle and have fallen into a caste system, and although I've told them to remain a democracy, they've gone monarchial. They've also tied steak knives around their hands and attacked the cats, who've resorted to throwing small flaming pieces of paper in return. I can't handle all the negativity and all the arguing. The dolls have even begun attacking me in my sleep, cutting my legs and my sheets.

I would like to go on a date somewhere nice. I am thirty one and you too may be thirty one or older, but not much younger.

* it's NOT ok to contact this poster with services or other commercial interests

PostingID: 419018480

To: pers-419018480@craigslist.org

Subject:

Date: Mon, 10 Sep 2007 14:46:30 -0700

From: ████████████

that's awesome, can I watch?

To: pers-419018480@craigslist.org

Subject: Looking for love - 31

Date: Mon, 10 Sep 2007 15:12:08 -0700

From: ████████████

How can cats build houses without thumbs?

Seriously.

To: pers-419018480@craigslist.org

Subject: Looking for love - 31

Date: Tue, 11 Sep 2007 21:44:38 -0700

From: ████████████

I admit, my mind boggles at the concept that someone has written a personal that comes off as being the most dysfunctional crazy cat lady ever. Yet I have to wonder, is this real or is this just really really well written by someone who's got a great imagination?

I'd like to learn more.

████

To: pers-419018480@craigslist.org
Subject: Looking for love - 31
Date: Tue, 11 Sep 2007 04:21:00 +0000
From: ███████████████

Hi Mary,

With me being only 3 credits shy of getting my minor in Psych, I feel qualified in making a non-professional assessment of your disorder! Many people suffer from the same disease...In many cases, it is cureable, but for some, it can be life long suffering. I am a nice self proclaimed Dr. and willing to take on challenges. If you would like to write me back and tell me more about yourself and your symptoms, maybe I can help cure you of this ailment?

███████

email this posting to a friend

please flag with care:
miscategorized
prohibited
spam/overpost
best of craigslist

Ex-convict seeking love

Reply to: pers-451358839@craigslist.org
Date: 2007-10-16, 11:45PM EDT

fore I begin Im a fit 32 year old blonde. Got a real nice body because
exercise was all I had to do in the can. Couple years back I got
convicted of killing my husband, but after a few appeals my lawyer
managed to get me out. And Im lovin the free life.

Im lookin for a nice guy to go out on a date with. We can take things
slow if youd like, but Im free and I need to have a man again. Id like to
meet a guy with a motorcycle who will take care of me.

* it's NOT ok to contact this poster with services or other commercial interests

PostingID: 451358839

To: pers-451358839@craigslist.org
Subject: thats great
Date: Wed, 17 Oct 2007 04:01:13 GMT
From: ████████████

Hi

loved the ad and Im sure I can take care of you...lol

so tell me more , I'm Intrigued!

████████

email this posting to a friend

please flag with care:
miscategorized
prohibited
spam/overpost
best of craigslist

My mother needs a date

Reply to: pers-451368356@craigslist.org
Date: 2007-10-16, 10:58PM CDT

My mother is 68 years old. Lately, she's been running around her house naked, painting the walls with ice cream and making sculptures with raw chicken. The other day, I found her gluing her silverware to the walls. She really needs to go out on a date.

You would ideally be a man aged 40-80. You'd have to be open-minded and athletic. She is in very good shape and a beautiful woman for her age. Forty percent of the time, she's a sweet, intelligent, creative and vibrant woman. The other sixty, she's mopping the floor with ketchup and chewing on aluminum foil.

Listen, I'll pay you to take her out on a date. Just, please make it happen. Please.

* it's NOT ok to contact this poster with services or other commercial interests

PostingID: 451368356

To: pers-451368356@craigslist.org
Subject: My mother needs a date
Date: Wed, 17 Oct 2007 05:56:33 -0700 (PDT)
From: ████████████████

my kind of woman..just looking for some one i can spend day time with...when i am home.i am a truck driver..pic on my profile..under the same name

---

To: pers-451368356@craigslist.org
Subject: about your mom's date
Date: Tue, 16 Oct 2007 21:41:31 -0700
From: ████████████████

can you send me your mom's pic ?

     thank you,

     ████████

email this posting to a friend

please flag with care:
miscategorized
prohibited
spam/overpost
best of craigslist

I would like to date a fat, balding, middle-aged man

Reply to: pers-454842907@craigslist.org
Date: 2007-10-20, 6:00PM EDT

I'm looking to date a fat, balding, middle-aged man with a dead end job and control issues. You would have to be in terrible shape, watch television all night, and be a borderline alcoholic. Special consideration will be given to those who can't control their anger, have children from a previous marriage, and drive a used car from the '80s. Terrible fashion sense is a must. Enormous debt desirable.

On our first date, you would take me somewhere dirty, insist that I drink cheap liquor all night, and shove your tongue down my throat. Extra points go to the first man who tells me he loves me within the first two hours of meeting me. After taking me home, you will insist on "coming in" and then you will attempt to have sex with me.

I'm especially attracted to men who have abused their former spouses, have a terrible relationship with their parents, and have health issues.

* it's NOT ok to contact this poster with services or other commercial interests

PostingID: 454842907

To: pers-454842907@craigslist.org
Subject: I would like to date a fat, balding, middle-aged man
Date: Sat, 20 Oct 2007 22:07:51 -0400
From: ██████████████

I'm all that plus a hard-drinking, hard-living lying son-of-a-bitch.

To: pers-454842907@craigslist.org
Subject: that's me!!!
Date: Sat, 20 Oct 2007 21:30:09 -0700 (PDT)
From: ██████████████

I'm a huge loser in both connotations of the word!!...I'm fat and I've always failed miserably at everything I've ever done...the only thing is that I don't have any kids from a previous marriage because I'm not very good with members of the opposite sex, after all not every woman values the qualities you're looking for and I have

██████████

email this posting to a friend

please flag with care:
miscategorized
prohibited
spam/overpost
best of craigslist

Picture This: A Perfect Date

Reply to: pers-401176179@craigslist.org
Date: 2007-08-19, 11:42PM CDT

I pick you up in my Mom's Chevy Truck and we head over to a nice
Noodles and Co-type place. You know, a nice restaurant. We get us
some food and then its off to the drag races. I'm a sucker for a race.
After that, we can even get some Dairy Queen. Then I think we should
maybe go to a lake or something.

It's really up to you, but I got me a raise at my second job so its time to
show a lady out the right way. With money.

* it's NOT ok to contact this poster with services or other commercial interests

PostingID: 401176179

To:	sale-401176179@craigslist.org
Subject:	I had to cringe....
Date:	Mon, 20 Aug 2007 07:27:24 -0700 (PDT)
From:	████████████

because I know someone, somewhere, REALLY does think that's the perfect date.

Ugh.

los angeles craigslist > central LA >
women seeking men

email this posting to a friend

please flag with care:
miscategorized
prohibited
spam/overpost
best of craigslist

I'd like to marry someone for their money

Reply to: pers-455802889@craigslist.org
Date: 2007-10-21, 6:48PM PDT

I'm an athletic, pretty, well educated 25 year old woman who is looking to marry someone for their money. You will ideally be a man of any age with a large home, a luxury car, and a killer job. Bonus points for those who have a vacation home or private land.

In return, I will turn a blind eye when you do something wrong (e.g. cheat on me, get caught doing hard drugs, or disappear for weeks at a time). We can have children, but you must give them everything they want and provide for them for the entirety of their lives.

Respond and I'll send you some of my model pictures.

* it's NOT ok to contact this poster with services or other commercial interests

PostingID: 455802889

To: pers-455802889@craigslist.org
Subject: I'd like to marry someone for their money
Date: Sun, 21 Oct 2007 19:25:25 -0700 (PDT)
From: ███████████████

hi.

MY NAME IS ████ AND I JUST SAW YOUR AD. CAN YOU SEND ME A FEW
OF YOUR PICS AND WE CAN GO FROM THEIR. U WILL BE MORE THEN
HAPPY IF YOU ARE FOR REAL. $10,000 be for and whole lot after that ... from
████████

To: pers-455802889@craigslist.org
Subject: I'd like to marry someone for their money
Date: Sun, 21 Oct 2007 19:48:11 -0700
From: ███████████████

Cool I got 13 cents

To: pers-455802889@craigslist.org
Subject: hello there. Seeking benefactor?
Date: Sun, 21 Oct 2007 19:38:57 -0700 (PDT)
From: ███████████████

You are a worthless sack of shit. If you were education, pretty, and all that, you
shouldnt be looking for some rich guy and blah blah blah. It shows how worthless
you are and how much of a gold-digger you are with no pride in anything you do. Go
fuck yourself.

What a loser... what guy with a million dollars would want trash like you? You are
a depreciating asset if someone were to marry yuou and give u everything u want?
Loser...

email this posting to a friend

please flag with care:
miscategorized
prohibited
spam/overpost
best of craigslist

Feminist seeking normal guy - 23

Reply to: pers-4219013995@craigslist.org
Date: 2007-09-10, 5:15PM EDT

Alright, first things first. I'm a feminist. I don't believe in the
subjugation of women, and I will not tolerate you doing anything
that oppresses or insults the female race. I believe that men have
had a reprehensible history of emotional and physical abuse toward
women and I hate most men because of it. I can't stand it when I see
a successful man walking down the street, only to be followed by his
female secretary, who he's certainly sexually harassing and oppressing.
I can't stand it when guys sit around watching football, talking about
what "chick" is "hot" and who they'd like to "tap." I don't believe in
dressing sexy or showing cleavage or drinking or doing drugs. I don't
agree with 90% of modern television or cinema, and I hate pop music
and its overt subjugation of teenage girls as sex items. In short, I am
not some ditzy babe you're gonna shlep, and I hate men.

That being said, I'm looking for a normal guy to go out on a date
with. I'm lonely and I'd like to have a meaningful relationship. All
my relationships with guys seem to fall apart and I can't figure it out.
Maybe you can help me.

* it's NOT ok to contact this poster with services or other commercial interests

PostingID: 4219013995

To: pers-4219013995@craigslist.org
Subject: Feminist seeking normal guy - 23
Date: Tue, 11 Sep 2007 08:50:58 -0700
From: ▓▓▓▓▓▓▓▓▓▓▓▓▓

feminists suck

To: pers-4219013995@craigslist.org
Subject: Feminist seeking normal guy - 23
Date: Mon, 10 Sep 2007 17:40:51 -0400
From: ▓▓▓▓▓▓▓▓▓▓▓▓

OK, I couldn't resist responding to your posting. Do you actually hate men or are you just posting flame bait? I can certainly appreciate feminism having been raised by avowed feminists. Then again, back then being a feminist meant being an egalitarian.

If you view yourself as an egalitarian and haven't actually condemned half of the human race as despicable, then I'd be more than happy to chat with you further. I tend to like equality and can certainly appreciate a strong woman who stands up for what she believes.

Seeking a callous, materialistic woman who hates her body

Reply to: pers-455796237@craigslist.org
Date: 2007-10-21, 6:38PM PDT

I'd like to date a cold, jaded, materialistic woman who hates her body and hates men. You would ideally be aged 21-35 with deep resentment toward males and your physique. You will preferably have lived off of your significant others since graduating college and not worked a day in your life. Potential candidates MUST prioritize material wealth above all else in a relationship. You will judge me based on my yearly salary and my social circle.

Although gorgeous, you must constantly complain about your body and call yourself fat. Priority will be given to women who ask me if they are fat at least twice a day and become offended when I complement you. Ideal candidates will work out to the point of obsession and have very likely developed an eating disorder.

We must argue constantly about everything and have sex infrequently. Your mood will ideally change every hour. You will hate me for the way your father treated you. I will, in turn, buy you whatever you want.

No fatties.

* it's NOT ok to contact this poster with services or other commercial interests

PostingID: 455796237

To: pers-455796237@craigslist.org
Subject: Is this a joke?
Date: Sun, 21 Oct 2007 20:27:21 -0700
From: ▓▓▓▓▓▓▓▓▓▓▓▓

I've just made myself vomit everything I ate for dinner and then I saw your listing on craigslist... then I started to wonder if you are the ex that I've dumped who asked me to pay back the money spent on my cartier. Pathetic.

If you could get me some chanel then I will think about dating a jerk like you.

Otherwise, fuck off, and shovel the money in your own ass.

To: pers-455796237@craigslist.org
Subject: Re: Seeking a callous, materialistic woman who hates her body
Date: Sun, 21 Oct 2007 18:48:58 -0700
From: ▓▓▓▓▓▓▓▓▓▓▓▓

I saw your ad on craigslist. I live in the Bay area. If you like my pic email me back and we can go on from there. Please send pics too.

email this posting to a friend

please flag with care:
miscategorized
prohibited
spam/overpost
best of craigslist

Cowgirl lookin fer her perfect Cowboy

Reply to: pers-416014343@craigslist.org
Date: 2007-09-06, 9:24PM PDT

Hello ma names judy. im a cowgirl plain and simple and im movin to los angeles to be near ma dyin cousin frank cause he dont have no one to watch after hisself. ma first husband bill boy was a real ccreep and he got hisself caught with a thirteen year old and ma second huband jimmy he was real abusive and an alkyholic so im leavin him for good and i want to find me a real cowboy to go out with. u better have a truck and some good lookin hats and we need to find us a good steak like the ones they serve down here at dennnys. if you think youre the guy give me something to read about yourself thanks judy

* it's NOT ok to contact this poster with services or other commercial interests

PostingID: 416014343

To: pers-416014343@craigslist.org
Subject: Yawn
Date: Thu, 6 Sep 2007 22:45:20 -0600
From: ███████████████

Wake me up when you want it doggie style.

To: pers-416014343@craigslist.org
Subject: RE
Date: Fri, 7 Sep 2007 00:46:15 EDT
From: ███████████████

How you doing? saw you on here and wanna get too know you....

Juggalette lookin for Juggalo in shining armor - 24

Reply to: pers-415076364@craigslist.org
Date: 2007-09-05, 11:12PM EDT

yo sup my names Lindsay. im a lifelong juggalette with the tats to
prove it and i live and breathe the wicked clown. wicked is my life
and i love all the psychopathic shit so if youre a juggalo and your cute
i want to go on a date somewhere nice, maybe to a ritzy place like
apllebees or somethin. i dont have a car and im gonna have to get my
baby jason a babysitter but its cool. i'm lookin for a real juggalo, none
of the pansy shit and no fakerz, you betta have the tats and the hair and
the jerseys to prove it.

* it's NOT ok to contact this poster with services or other commercial interests

PostingID: 415076364

To: pers-415076364@craigslist.org
Subject: hi from cl
Date: Thu, 6 Sep 2007 00:26:36 -0400
From: ▮▮▮▮▮▮▮▮▮▮▮

i have a clown on my back with a mask and an axe, skull on my left arm medium built. short blk hair 5'9 a bit cute fun person i would say.

can send you pick if you reply and i have a car prelude 99. 26 years old

---

To: pers-415076364@craigslist.org
Subject: Juggalette lookin for juggalo in shining armor - 24
Date: Thu, 6 Sep 2007 07:24:02 GMT
From: ▮▮▮▮▮▮▮▮▮▮▮

oh!
Shit baby my middle name is freak!
you got my spook ruhght and if get to you I will raise your bugaloo for some shit and fun with you!

Dude u date!

To: pers-415076364@craigslist.org
Subject: Juggalette lookin for juggalo in shining armor - 24
Date: Thu, 6 Sep 2007 00:27:53 -0400
From: ▮▮▮▮▮▮▮▮▮▮▮

"yo-sup"!!?? ritzy place = Applebee's !!??
Good grief. What a prize.

To: pers-415076364@craigslist.org
Subject: Best troll CL post ever
Date: Thu, 6 Sep 2007 03:01:25 -0400
From: ▮▮▮▮▮▮▮▮▮▮▮

The Applebees part is classic.
Whoever you are, you win the internet.

[106 | Wanted: Bear Cubs for My Children]

email this posting to a friend

please flag with care:
miscategorized
prohibited
spam/overpost
best of craigslist

Promiscuous 28F looking for meaningful relationship

Reply to: pers-402882533@craigslist.org
Date: 2007-08-21, 8:09PM PDT

Hi guys. I'm a 28 year old white woman, brown hair, shapely but fit, shortish (5'6). I've been around town and am sick of the dating scene. What I'm looking for is a meaningful relationship that could lead to something greater, like marriage and children. I'm a very honest person. So I'll come out and say it: I've slept with over two hundred men.

This is not because I am a slut or a sex addict. When I was younger, I just wanted to express myself through sexuality, rather than music or arts or writing or whatever. In the past few years, I've only been with twenty men, which is very low.

I haven't been checked for STDs but I'm sure that everything is alright (I always use protection and nothing seems to be funky down there).

Will you take me out?

If you reply ill send pics, i'm not comfortable posting them on here

* it's NOT ok to contact this poster with services or other commercial interests

PostingID: 402882533

To: pers-402882533@craigslist.org
Subject: Promiscuous 28F looking for meaningful relationship
Date: Thu, 23 Aug 2007 19:16:00 EDT
From: ▓▓▓▓▓▓▓▓▓▓▓

would you fuck a 37 yr old handsome millionaire?i like women who have been
around like you because i thust them.

To: pers-402882533@craigslist.org
Subject: pics for later then :)
Date: Thu, 23 Aug 2007 19:16:00 EDT
From: ▓▓▓▓▓▓▓▓▓▓▓

hey say i'm cute sometimes hot :) so i'n sending the pic not because i'm afraid of
how i look like its just because 'i waiti till i see u first

about me i slept with only one girl . sounds creasy!!!

and my way of having fun is to be stable and have someone secial sides me , like a
wif or a gf but i've allways been comitted to the relationship

i dont care about the past but if im gonna be u r guy ad he only thats enough

---

To: pers-402882533@craigslist.org
Subject: Promiscuous 28F looking for meaningful relationship
Date: Tue, 21 Aug 2007 21:38:59 -0700 (PDT)
From: ▓▓▓▓▓▓▓▓▓▓▓

It sounds like you've had some sexual issues back when you were a kid - sex will
never solve your problems.

Chapter 5: Free Stuff

A true story: I spent weeks conceptualizing absurd things that no rational human being would ever want—haunted dolls, moldy food, Pauly Shore memorabilia, merkins (pubic wigs)—and posted them all online as "Free Stuff." The response was overwhelming—I regularly got hundreds of e-mails from people who desperately wanted my wares. Some became so attached, they continued to email for weeks, and to these individuals I apologize: I don't really own a two hundred foot tall American flag, or a mummy, or even a gun that shoots bees.

email this posting to a friend

please flag with care:
miscategorized
prohibited
spam/overpost
best of craigslist

Free Armoire

Reply to: sale-397224456@craigslist.org
Date: 2007-08-14, 8:44PM EDT

My wife and I found an armoire in an alley behind our church last weekend. Being an antique lover, she immediately fell for it. It is from the late 19th century (she thinks), with intricately carved designs and six shelves. It's made of walnut (that's what she said). One of our friends said that it is extremely rare and we could sell it for several thousands.

We were going to keep it but we now think the armoire is haunted. My wife found a message carved under one of the shelves about a pox and there's a giant pentagram carved on the very bottom (out of view and doesn't affect the overall look) with a bunch of latin words. Also, when we first got it, there were some red stains on the bottom shelf, but my wife cleaned them because she thought they were Kool-Aid or some sort of juice.

Ever since we brought it into our house, she's been really scared at night. One time, our lamp fell over (I think it was because of the wind) and our daughter came down with a little cold, but that's all. She thinks we need to give it away to someone who can either deal with the "curse" or can make it holy again. I just wish I could keep it (because it is truly beautiful), but she won't let me.

Free to anyone who can come pick it up. I'll also take a six pack if you got that.

* it's NOT ok to contact this poster with services or other commercial interests

PostingID: 397224456

[110 I Wanted: Bear Cubs for My Children]

To: sale-397224456@craigslist.org
Subject: Free Armoire
Date: Tue, 14 Aug 2007 22:29:53 -0700 (PDT)
From: ███████████

ill take the dreeser and the ghost wo will welcome them to our home please let me know thank you

---

To: sale-397224456@craigslist.org
Subject: Free Armoire
Date: Tue, 14 Aug 2007 21:05:08 -0400
From: ███████████

The piece is beautiful. Have you considered having a Roman Catholic priest to bless your house and all the belongings in it? What does it say in Latin? A priest could tell you and confirm what the image is on

the bottom of the piece. Be not afraid, nothing is greater than God.

███████

To: sale-397224456@craigslist.org
Subject: Free Armoire
Date: Wed, 15 Aug 2007 07:36:15 -0400
From: ███████████

Dear,friend my is ed &L AM a bo rn again christian,which means thayyor
t I am fill with the holy spirtGOD H.S I LIVE near york &northren p.way if you still have if it ,it could very well be demon posses.I was a antique dealer so if you will call me at ███████ I think I can help you one way or another.

To: sale-397224456@craigslist.org
Subject: armoire
Date: Wed, 14 Aug 2007 19:59:42 -0700 (PDT)
From: ███████████████

Good evening; I frequent a lot of second hand stores and craigslist. I use a Native American ritual called smudging; its like Lysol. If you wife is willing to try you may be able to keep the item.

Items needed: White sage smudge stick or loose white sage with charcoal and something to hold the charcoal and sage that would allow you to smudge the armoire.

I would light my sage and allow the smoke to fill the room and go around the item and inside the drawers underneath etc. Since the item has been in your home you can smoke the entire house. While I am smoking I pray to the Creator to remove any negative energy from this item and may it be a blessing to my home. I hope this helps.. ███████████████

To: sale-397224456@craigslist.org
Subject: Free Armoire
Date: Wed, 15 Aug 2007 13:51:40 -0700 (PDT)
From: ███████████████

Hi,   It is about armoir that is "haunted". I can pick it up because I know how to deal with the occult...

For the 6 pack, I will give you a free psychic reading.... My phone is ███████████.

███████

email this posting to a friend

Free Extremely Rare Star Wars Action Figures

Reply to: sale-413238856@craigslist.org
Date: 2007-09-03, 11:00PM EDT

Let me preface this by stating that I spent a good fifteen years of my life collecting these Star Wars toys. There are ten for free here, and a few of them are considered extremely rare, including a vinyl-caped Jawa that usually sells for about $700 dollars and a red lava Darth Vader. I loved these toys, but I can't stand to look at them anymore. This is because my mastiff swallowed them, and passed them onto my couch.

They're still sitting on the couch as he left them. Free to anyone who wants to come pick them up.

* it's NOT ok to contact this poster with services or other commercial interests

PostingID: 413238856

To: sale-413238856@craigslist.org
Subject: Free Extremely Rare Star Wars Action Figures
Date: Mon, 3 Sep 2007 21:42:23 -0700 (PDT)
From: ▇▇▇▇▇▇▇▇▇▇

dont mean to be blunt but i dont kno wat a mastiff is but what your telling me is that
u have collectible star wars figurines covered in shit?

To: sale-413238856@craigslist.org
Subject:
Date: Mon, 3 Sep 2007 21:42:23 -0700 (PDT)
From: ▇▇▇▇▇▇▇▇▇▇

Did you wash them or they are still there I mean after he defecated ? If you cleaned
them (with soap at least) I would love to take them off your hands

▇▇▇▇▇

To: sale-413238856@craigslist.org
Subject: a bit of dog poop
Date: Mon, 3 Sep 2007 23:36:00 -0400
From: ▇▇▇▇▇▇▇▇▇▇

that doesn't bother me,

they will go nicely with the few of the ones i got,

i'll gladly come by and get em off your couch....

i am sorry this happened to you

To: sale-413238856@craigslist.org
Subject: Free Extremely Rare Star Wars Action Figures
Date: Tue, 04 Sep 2007 08:08:06 -0400
From: ███████████████

Sorry ! To read about this misfortune . Funny but than not so funny . Be easy on your pet . He must have been feeling neglected . Perhaps that is why he tenderly nibbled on them. (TOYS)<<< Have a great day !

>>>

To: sale-413238856@craigslist.org
Subject: star wars toys
Date: Tue, 4 Sep 2007 00:14:59 -0400
From: ███████████████

are these like, in at least good condition still (poo aside)? also where is this located?

email this posting to a friend

please flag with care:
miscategorized
prohibited
spam/overpost
best of craigslist

Free Children's Halloween Costumes

Reply to: sale-455815212@craigslist.org
Date: 2007-10-21, 7:04PM PDT

I work at a costume warehouse. We are looking to clean out our space and make room for some new 2007 costumes. The following costumes are for children, and have been sitting in our warehouse for years, collecting dust:

1.) Donnie Osmond from "The Osmonds"
2.) Malcom X with fake glasses and Nation of Islam suit
3.) Bettie Page with cute tiger skin bikini, red lipstick, and fake eyelashes
4.) Baby from "Dinosaurs" television show, with "Not the mama" voice activation
5.) Baby Adolph Hitler with fake mustache
6.) Elvira with low cut black dress and fake breasts
7.) Baby Rush Limbaugh

All the above costumes are free for pickup.

* it's NOT ok to contact this poster with services or other commercial interests

Posting ID: 455815212

To: sale-455815212@craigslist.org
Subject: costumes
Date: Mon, 22 Oct 2007 11:04:09 -0400
From: ▇▇▇▇▇▇▇▇▇▇▇

I- have two kids one is 4 months and the other is 9.

we are interested in the baby hitler and the elvira or malcolm X

can we see them if they are still there?

thanks

▇▇▇▇

▇▇▇▇▇▇▇

To: sale-455815212@craigslist.org
Subject: Free Children's Halloween Costumes
Date: Sun, 21 Oct 2007 22:22:46 -0700
From: ▇▇▇▇▇▇▇▇▇▇▇

Elvira with low cut black dress and fake breasts

do u still have this

email this posting to a friend

please flag with care:
miscategorized
prohibited
spam/overpost
best of craigslist

Our house exploded and whatever is left is free

Reply to: sale-419038426@craigslist.org
Date: 2007-09-10, 5:41PM EDT

We had a lab in the basement that exploded while we were out of town and there's still a lot of things left in the rubble. We can't go back because of the cops. If you want some free stuff, I'll give you an address. I'm pretty sure theres a ton of DVDs, some kitchenware, a metal file cabinet, a bunch of tools, whatever, its all yours, dude.

* it's NOT ok to contact this poster with services or other commercial interests

PostingID: 419038426

[118 | Wanted: Bear Cubs for My Children]

To: sale-419038426@craigslist.org
Subject: craigslist posting...
Date: Mon, 10 Sep 2007 18:04:21 -0400
From: ████████████

Uhmm.. Yeah, you can't post that, you're going to get someone arrested. It's called looting and it's illegal, even with the owners permission. And if you had a lab in the basement chances are the cops are gonna think anyone that goes over there is involved... Just an FYI

To: sale-419038426@craigslist.org
Subject: Our house exploded and whatever is left is free
Date: Mon, 10 Sep 2007 18:02:16 -0400
From: ████████████

yo whats the address?

████

To: sale-419038426@craigslist.org
Subject:
Date: Mon, 10 Sep 2007 15:11:38 -0700
From: ████████████

were u making drugs or something? what is the address?

email this posting to a friend

please flag with care:
miscategorized
prohibited
spam/overpost
best of craigslist

Free antique mannequin

Reply to: sale-401997747@craigslist.org
Date: 2007-08-20, 9:45PM CDT

I got this old mannequin in my garage that moves around at night. She wasn't always like this but about six months ago I came home from a bar and there she was, on the driveway, nude as a newborn. No one could have put here there because I live alone, and no one broke in. Then, four months ago, I heard some rustling out there and I went to check it out. Thought it was a raccoon because they'd lived in my attic before. But it was her. She was rolling around all by herself.

* it's NOT ok to contact this poster with services or other commercial interests

PostingID: 401997747

To: sale-401997747@craigslist.org
Subject: mannequin
Date: Mon, 20 Aug 2007 21:25:34 -0700 (PDT)
From: ███████████████

I would like this mannequin and whatever drugs you're on please

---

To: sale-401997747@craigslist.org
Subject: craigslist mannequin
Date: Wed, 22 Aug 2007 18:11:01 -0500
From: ███████████████

i need this mannequin please let me know if you still have it. it would be perfect for my kids to play with and to babysit them.

thanks ██████

To: sale-401997747@craigslist.org
Subject: re: mannequin
Date: Tue, 21 Aug 2007 08:49:19 -0500
From: ███████████████

Hi, I'm interested in the mannequin you listed on craigslist. I am always on the look out for the paranormal. This is such a great find in our great state of OK! Please let me know where I can pick this up and if I will need any equipment (nets, potions, my talisman, etc.). Thanks!

To: sale-401997747@craigslist.org
Subject: Free antique mannequin
Date: Fri, 24 Aug 2007 15:29:04 -0500
From: ███████████████

i need a Free antique
mannequin i can pickup you
can call me ██████████
██████ thanks ██████

email this posting to a friend

please flag with care:
miscategorized
prohibited
spam/overpost
best of craigslist

Free kick in the face

Reply to: sale-454857696@craigslist.org
Date: 2007-10-20, 6:19PM EDT

Who wants some?

Bring it.

* it's NOT ok to contact this poster with services or other commercial interests

PostingID: 454857696

To: sale-454857696@craigslist.org
Subject: Free kick in the face
Date: Sat, 20 Oct 2007 18:48:49 -0400
From: ▮▮▮▮▮▮▮▮▮▮

I'll take it

email this posting to a friend

please flag with care:
miscategorized
prohibited
spam/overpost
best of craigslist

Free: Unbelievably Ugly Chair (with surprises inside)

Reply to: sale-399143799@craigslist.org
Date: 2007-08-17, 7:13AM PDT

I'm posting this for my mother, who, bless her soul, is too ill to access her GMail. We have a chair that is an abomination. It is the ugliest, most foul piece of furniture I have ever set eyes upon, and we want to get rid of it—quick! The chair has, throughout its lifespan, been used as a bed, toilet, plate, punching bag and operation table. My sister broke her water over the chair and I have had stitches twice because of the chair. It's seen its fair share of vomit, feces, food and cigarette butts. The chair has witnessed one tragedy after another in the twenty years we've owned it, and we need to get it out of here.

I know, at this point, you're asking, "Why would I want such a piece of junk" The answer is simple: WE'VE PUT TREASURES IN THE CUSHIONS. Yes, treasures. Why would we put treasures in the chair? Because we want it gone, and we don't want to touch it. What are the treasures, you ask? Are they good treasures? Are they magical?

Well, they're not magical. But they are EXTREMELY VALUABLE. These are things my mother inherited. Some are family heirlooms. Some are pocket change. There could be anything in those cushions.

For those who want to brave it out, this is the couch/treasure trove you've been looking for. First come, first served.

* it's NOT ok to contact this poster with services or other commercial interests

PostingID: 399143799

To: sale-399143799@craigslist.org
Subject: chair
Date: Fri, 17 Aug 2007 08:20:07 -0700 (PDT)
From: ███████████████

this is not a "piece of junk!" it sounds like a NASTY piece of trash! good lord, i hope u find someone who would take it for the "treasure" inside

---

To: sale-399143799@craigslist.org
Subject: Free: Unbelievably Ugly Chair (with surprises inside)
Date: Fri, 17 Aug 2007 08:30:41 -0700
From: ███████████████

ok i'll bite email me back were i can go for this wonderful ugly sick nasty chair it sounds like what i been looking for might give it to my mother in law lol thanks

please flag with care:
miscategorized
prohibited
spam/overpost
best of craigslist

Free Edible Flags

Reply to: <u>sale-xbcbq-1084363553@craigslist.org</u>
Date: 2009-03-20, 5:32PM CDT

I have a garage full of edible American flags that were developed in 1999 by Hanzbrucker Foods. The box reads:

"These beautiful flags look, feel, and waver like traditional polyester Stars 'n' Stripes, but with one noticeable difference—they're entirely edible! Imagine your neighbor's surprise as you walk outside to get your newspaper and take a bite out of Old Glory! Or, imagine shocking your mother by serving an American flag for Christmas dinner! These flags can be used as spectacular pranks or delicious snacks! Past uses have included:

1.) American flag meatloaf with potatoes au gratin and grilled asparagus.
2.) The edible march of Paul Revere.
3.) The raising of—and devouring of—the American flag at basketball, baseball and football games.
4.) The placing of—and devouring of—the American flag beside a tombstone.

And more!"

I'm not sure if these have expired or not. They're in the original shrink wrapping. I have three hundred cases.

* it's NOT ok to contact this poster with services or other commercial interests

PostingID: 1084363553

To: sale-xbcbq-1084363553@craigslist.org
Date: Sat, 21 Mar 2009 12:06 AM
Subject: Free Edible Flags
From: ▮▮▮▮▮▮▮▮▮▮▮▮

1999 THEY ARE EXPIRED

To: sale-xbcbq-1084363553@craigslist.org
Subject: Free Edible Flags
Date: Fri, 20 Mar 2009 11:50 PM
From: ▮▮▮▮▮▮▮▮▮▮▮▮

wow I want some, really kewl!!!

To: sale-xbcbq-1084363553@craigslist.org
Subject: edible flags
Date: Fri, 20 Mar 2009 10:45 PM
From: ▮▮▮▮▮▮▮▮▮▮▮▮

I would like the edible flags. I'll keep one or two, and give the rest to a cub scout pack. I think they'd have fun with that.

▮▮▮▮▮

email this posting to a friend

please flag with care:
miscategorized
prohibited
spam/overpost
best of craigslist

Free Christmas Ornaments

Reply to: sale-455779460@craigslist.org
Date: 2007-10-21, 6:15PM PDT

My husband Don works at a latex company that manufactures adult
toys. Last year, they filled a gigantic order of penis and vagina
Christmas ornaments that ended up falling through. They've had these
cute little Christmas penises sitting around their warehouse since last
December. They were going to throw them away, but I thought, "maybe
someone will want these." Do you?

There are many different models:

* Small, hairless penis with a red light bulb in the urethra
* Small, hairless vagina with a red light bulb as the clitoris
* "Santa Claus" penis with a white beard and a cute little hat
* The "Three Wise Penises" with a baby Christ penis nativity set
* An "Angel" Vagina Tree Topper with a white dress
* And more!

These ornaments are first come, first served!

* it's NOT ok to contact this poster with services or other commercial interests

PostingID: 455779460

To: sale-455779460@craigslist.org

Subject: Free Christmas Ornaments

Date: Sun, 21 Oct 2007 18:37:18 -0700 (PDT)

From: ████████████

hi I am interested in your ornaments if they are still avalible please reply thank you.

████

please flag with care:
miscategorized
prohibited
spam/overpost
best of craigslist

Free Mummy

Reply to: sale-399610126@craigslist.org
Date: 2007-08-17, 7:30PM EDT

When I was a young child, my father owned a traveling carnival. He passed, leaving behind countless curiosities and an estate to my older brother. To me, he left a mummy. I don't know if it is real or not, but I think it may be. I'm not going to touch it, much less unwrap it. We never really got along, and I guess this was his way of having the last laugh.

I don't want the mummy. Do you? Free to anyone who can pick it up (it comes in a big wooden box).

* it's NOT ok to contact this poster with services or other commercial interests

PostingID: 399610126

To: sale-399610126@craigslist.org
Subject: Free Mummy
Date: Sat, 18 Aug 2007 11:19:12 -0500
From: ▮▮▮▮▮▮▮▮▮

Mummies depending upon where they originate may have value. I would call up a local museum and see if they would want to buy it or in the worse case you donate it and take a tax write off.

Regards,

▮▮▮▮

▮▮▮▮▮▮

▮▮▮▮▮

▮▮▮▮▮

To: sale-399610126@craigslist.org
Subject: Free Mummy
Date: Sat, 18 Aug 2007 12:14:40 -0400
From: ▮▮▮▮▮▮▮▮▮▮

Shit I'll take it I love that sick morbid stuff, hopefully it's not gone already. Where are you located?

▮▮▮▮▮

To: sale-399610126@craigslist.org
Subject: Free Mummy
Date: Sat, 18 Aug 2007 14:20:35 EDT
From: ▮▮▮▮▮▮▮▮▮▮

you should call a musuem, or you have Space Farms up in Sussex also, they would display it with your name donated by if you want that? I dont think you can just give a mummy away? because it is considered a corpse. Sorry to hear your Dad treated you like that.

▮▮▮▮▮

ok, this sounds like the start of a bad horror movie, but yes, I would like the mummy. Where is he?

Free antique bisque doll

Reply to: sale-401994737@craigslist.org
Date: 2007-08-20, 10:40PM EDT

She was given to me in 1940 by my grandfather, a German dollmaker. She has beautiful brown hair and I've always loved her. She lied to me about several things and I can't look at her anymore. First, she took kitty's purse and I can't tolerate that. After that, she hurt kitty and she's still stained from it. She even hurt daddy.

Would make an ideal gift for a young girl.

* it's NOT ok to contact this poster with services or other commercial interests

PostingID: 401994737

[132 | Wanted: Bear Cubs for My Children]

To: sale-401994737@craigslist.org
Subject: Free antique bisque doll
Date: Tue, 21 Aug 2007 17:44:38 EDT
From: ███████████████

ARE YOU SURE YOU DIDN'T TAKE KITTY'S PURSE AND HURT DADDY? AND
IF THIS DOLL IS SO EVIL WHY WOULD IT MAKE SUCH AN IDEAL GIFT FOR A
YOUNG GIRL?

To: sale-401994737@craigslist.org
Subject: strange
Date: Tue, 21 Aug 2007 09:51:20 -0400
From: ███████████████

your ad is very wierd and i dont know anyone who would give that doll

to

there daughter after you write suck strange things...

think about it...

To: sale-401994737@craigslist.org
Subject: sale-401994737@craigslist.org
Date: Mon, 20 Aug 2007 20:37:15 -0700 (PDT)
From: ███████████████

Please let me know if still available, my six year old daughter would love to have it.

Thanks,

Regards

███████

email this posting to a friend

please flag with care:
miscategorized
prohibited
spam/overpost
best of craigslist

Free Rack

Reply to: sale-417395206@craigslist.org
Date: 2007-09-08, 4:01PM CDT

My grandfather passed a couple of weeks ago and I found this rack in his basement. It was a homemade rack and it's still in good condition. It's a bit stained, but nothing that you can't wash off with some bleach and elbow grease. My wife won't let me keep it (and trust me, sometimes I wish I could put my kids on this thing!), so I'm going to give it away to the first person who replies and picks it up.

* it's NOT ok to contact this poster with services or other commercial interests

PostingID: 417395206

[134 | Wanted: Bear Cubs for My Children]

To: sale-417395206@craigslist.org
Subject: Free Rack
Date: Sat, 8 Sep 2007 15:16:36 -0700 (PDT)
From: ███████████████

Hello I would like to have your rack.

██████ Cell ██████████

home ████████████

please let me know one way or the other if it is sold please. Thank you

---

To: sale-417395206@craigslist.org
Subject: Free Rack
Date: Sat, 8 Sep 2007 19:25:55 EDT
From: ███████████████

please let me know if you still have it thanks █████

email this posting to a friend

please flag with care:
miscategorized
prohibited
spam/overpost
best of craigslist

Ronald Regan Tortilla

Reply to: sale-pvmfr-1085630151@craigslist.org
Date: 2009-03-21, 3:08PM CDT

My roommate Gary works for Burrito Palace as a burrito artist. He's got this wicked collection of tortillas with skillet-burned celebrity faces. A couple weeks ago I accidentally used his Ronald Regan tortilla to make a giant taco and realized halfway through that I was chewing on Ronnie's forehead.

I put it back together the best I could. It's a little gnawed up. Would look great in a picture frame!

Free to the first person who wants to come pick it up.

* it's NOT ok to contact this poster with services or other commercial interests

PostingID: 1085630151

To: sale-pvmfr-1085630151@craigslist.org
Subject: Tortilla
Date: Sat, 21 Mar 2009 8:43 PM
From: ███████████████

I would like it, is it still available? Can I get to your location on the DART bus?

[136 | Wanted: Bear Cubs for My Children]

email this posting to a friend

please flag with care:
miscategorized
prohibited
spam/overpost
best of craigslist

Free Book Collection

Reply to: sale-419035129@craigslist.org
Date: 2007-09-10, 5:38PM EDT

Inherited from my Egyptian ancestors, this collection of ancient spells
and underworld secrets is free to the first person who can come pick it
up. My wife is sick of the smell; the books are bound by human skin
and contain ancient writing etched in blood. There are seven books in
all. They are quite ugly but a great conversation piece nonetheless.

* it's NOT ok to contact this poster with services or other commercial interests

PostingID: 419035129

To: sale-419035129@craigslist.org
Subject: Egyptian book Collection
Date: Mon, 10 Sep 2007 14:54:29 -0700 (PDT)
From: ██████████████

Hello,

I will come pickup thebooks immediately. Where are you located. please call me
██████████████

To: sale-419035129@craigslist.org
Subject: Free Book Collection
Date: Tue, 11 Sep 2007 03:02:39 EDT
From: ██████████████

interrested in books please call ██████████

email this posting to a friend

please flag with care:
miscategorized
prohibited
spam/overpost
best of craigslist

Free Nugs

Reply to: comm-397234876@craigslist.org
Date: 2007-08-14, 6:57PM MDT

Free nugs for anyone who wants to hang out with me and Stephanie and watch South Park. We got all kinds of shit (even Halo) and my buddy Will said he'd bring the Doritos. Just looking for some new friends to trip out with, that's all. We're totally chill.

* it's NOT ok to contact this poster with services or other commercial interests

PostingID: 397234876

To: comm-397234876@craigslist.org
Subject: dude
Date: Thu, 16 Aug 2007 21:46:18 -0400
From: ███████████████

where do i sign?

To: comm-397234876@craigslist.org
Subject: cl ad
Date: Wed, 15 Aug 2007 16:23:55 -0700
From: ███████████████

I read your ad and it sounds like fun. I just moved here from Tucson a couple weeks ago. I am also chill. I like South Park and drugs and dorritos.

You should email me back or call ████████ if you would like to hangout.

████████

To: comm-397234876@craigslist.org
Subject: nugs? did someone say nugs?
Date: Wed, 15 Aug 2007 21:22:48 -0600
From: ███████████████

ya, i'm ██████, would love to hang out. 23. sorry, i'm a guy. i hope you don't care but i love southpark and halo...peace

email this posting to a friend

please <u>flag</u> with care:
<u>miscategorized</u>
<u>prohibited</u>
<u>spam/overpost</u>
<u>best of craigslist</u>

Free: Antique Mirror

Reply to: <u>sale-398637840@craigslist.org</u>
Date: 2007-08-16, 3:32PM EDT

My sister recently inherited a gigantic antique mirror. It's quite beautiful. It was my mother's, and she was very excited to put it in her living room. She now wants to give it away. Here's why:

The mirror came from my mother's grandmother, Zora, who lived as a traveling mystic. She reportedly took the mirror from a hermetic Cuban antique collector in exchange for his fate (according to the cards). We know this because she left a diary entry detailing her acquisition of the mirror (typed out below).

"September 12th, 1902

In Havana, read the cards of a queer older antiquist named Javier. He lived in his shop, surrounded by curiosities and possessed many rare and magical items. I begged him to part with his shrunken skulls and canine collections, but he would not. Nor would he sell me what he claimed was a page from the original bible. Having heard of my reputation as a master soothsayer, he finally agreed to an exchange: his fate for an enchanted mirror.

The mirror, he claimed, had been given to him by a slave trader who'd given two men for a full furniture set in South Africa. After setting the mirror in the bathroom of his cargo ship, two deck swabbies quickly fell mad and jumped overboard. It was said that, thereafter, all who looked into the mirror came under some sort of affliction or lost any sense they once possessed.

I gladly took the mirror, and have never once laid eyes upon its glass"

This mirror was kept in my mother's attic, covered in thick cloth, until her death. It's very large (likely six feet or more in height and three or four in width). We believe it may have some gold encasing, as the frame is quite luxurious. We've only seen the back of it. We were told as kids to never look at the glass side. Out of good conscience, we'd like to not sell it, and we'd also like to not destroy it.

Free for whoever can pick it up.

PostingID: 398637840

To: sale-398637840@craigslist.org
Subject: MIRROR
Date: Thu, 16 Aug 2007 12:51:47 -0700 (PDT)
From: ▇▇▇▇▇▇▇▇▇

DUE YOU STILL HAVE THE MIRROR I WOULD LIKE TO HAVE THE MIRROR.
YOU CAN EMAIL ME BACK.

THANK YOU

▇▇▇▇

To: sale-398637840@craigslist.org
Subject: Free: Antique Mirror
Date: Thu, 16 Aug 2007 16:54:04 -0400
From: ▇▇▇▇▇▇▇

DO YOU STILL HAVE THIS MIRROR I DON'T BELIEVE IN THESE THINGS AND
LOVE ANTIQUES BUT COULD NEVER AFFORD ONE. PLS LET ME KNOW!

THANK YOU!

To: sale-398637840@craigslist.org
Subject: mirrow
Date: Fri, 17 Aug 2007 01:50:38 +0000
From: ▇▇▇▇▇▇▇▇

can you have someone take a pic before I drive out there and get it,,I really would
like to see a pic of this first I have a truck and some men to pick up,,,that I have to
pay the men so that is why is it important to see a pic first,,,hope you understand if
you don't want to look at the mirrow itself have a neighbor or friend or someone that
is not supersious take the pic,,,,ps..I hope this curse doesn't follow to me thanks

email this posting to a friend

please flag with care:
miscategorized
prohibited
spam/overpost
best of craigslist

Free Two Hundred Foot Tall American Flag

Reply to: sale-mkegu-1084399838@craigslist.org
Date: 2009-03-20, 5:57PM CDT

My neighbor got one that's fifty feet and I wanted to show him who was boss, so I had a two hundred foot tall flag made. It waves beautifully in the wind, but it's so big that it covers my entire house and part of my neighbor's house, so I need to get rid of it.

You'll probably need a really, really, really, really, really big truck.

* it's NOT ok to contact this poster with services or other commercial interests

PostingID: 1084399838

[144 | Wanted: Bear Cubs for My Children]

To: sale-mkegu-1084399838@craigslist.org
Subject: flag for real
Date: Sat, 21 Mar 2009 2:57 AM
From: ███████████████

I WANT IT AND WILL MOUNT IT IF YOU STILL HAVE IT. ████.HAVE
TRUCK,WILL PIC UP[.

To: sale-mkegu-1084399838@craigslist.org
Subject: Free Two Hundred Foot Tall American Flag
Date: Sat, 21 Mar 2009 1:13 AM
From: ██████████████████

HELLO,

NOTICED YOUR AD ON CRAIGS LIST, IF YOU STILL HAVE THE FLAG WOULD
YOU PLEASE LET ME KNOW, WE ARE BUILDING A SMALL TOWN AND COULD
REALLY USE IT. IF YOU WOULD LIKE TO CALL THAT'S FINE ██████████ IF NO
ANSWER, PLEASE LEAVE MESSAGE WE WORK OUTSIDE ALOT BUILDING
COMING IN AND OUT FOR MESSAGES.

MANY THANKS,

████████ AND ██████

To: sale-mkegu-1084399838@craigslist.org
Subject: Free Two Hundred Foot Tall American Flag
Date: Sat, 21 Mar 2009 5:03 AM
From: ███████████████

MY FATHER WOULD LOVE THIS! DO YOU STILL HAVE IT? HE HAS RANCH.
████

email this posting to a friend

please flag with care:
miscategorized
prohibited
spam/overpost
best of craigslist

Free Dinosaur Skeleton

Reply to: sale-401151848@craigslist.org
Date: 2007-08-19, 10:54PM CDT

Me and Willy were diggin in his pappas backyard and we found a full dinosaur skeleton. We wanted to sell it but now we just wanna give it away becaus its takin up allof Willys garage. I think its one of them bigger dinasors? There must be hundreds of bones here. The skull is really cool lookin

Come and get it its free but youll need a truck for sure

* it's NOT ok to contact this poster with services or other commercial interests

PostingID: 401151848

To: sale-401151848@craigslist.org
Subject: Dinosaur
Date: Sun, 19 Aug 2007 21:31:07 -0700 (PDT)
From: ████████████

I'll tako it.

████████

To: sale-401151848@craigslist.org
Subject: dino skeleton
Date: Sun, 19 Aug 2007 21:20:01 -0700 (PDT)
From: ████████████

if you have dino bones exspeically a whole skeleton. you should get ahold of the right ppl.

they might be but it from you!!

email this posting to a friend

please flag with care:
miscategorized
prohibited
spam/overpost
best of craigslist

Free rent (not a scam)

Reply to: sale-397203663@craigslist.org
Date: 2007-08-14, 7:23PM CDT

Alright here's the deal. My dad's lazy and he needs someone around in case he falls over or gets hurt. He's big, really big. He usually wears a huge undershirt and swim trunks. He can barely walk but he won't let me get him any caretakers. So if you want to live somewhere for free, his basement is perfect. There's a bunch of canned food down there from the '50s and we used to have an Atari but it broke. There's a bed. It's sort of filthy on the walls. If you want it clean you'll have to clean it yourself. The rent is free, and this is not a caretaker position. You really don't have to do much, just listen for if he's screaming.

Just make sure that Dad's alright from time to time, and if you hear him fall over, help him get back up because he can't do it himself. He falls over sometimes onto tables or couches because he's always drinking. I can't be there for him because I live in a different state.

He orders chicken and pizza every day so you won't have to cook for him and you don't even really have to hang out with him, because he doesn't like people. He has a few old bloodhounds to keep him company. There's a basement door to the outside so you don't have to walk through the house everytime you come or go.

Sometimes he has his friend Hank over and they get rowdy and break stuff. So he has all these broken tables and televisions all over the house, and there's a hole in the floor where he can peek down into the basement to scare you. But if you want I can leave you some wood to cover up the hole.

* it's NOT ok to contact this poster with services or other commercial interests

PostingID: 397203663

[148 | Wanted: Bear Cubs for My Children]

To: sale-397203663@craigslist.org
Subject: basement room
Date: Wed, 15 Aug 2007 12:41:07 -0500
From: ███████████████

Your post was absurd, however I might know some folks that would be suitable for this arrangement.

What's the square footage of this basement?

To: sale-397203663@craigslist.org
Subject: Free rent (not a scam)
Date: Wed, 15 Aug 2007 21:07:51 EDT
From: ███████████████

where vis this im interested

email this posting to a friend

please flag with care:
miscategorized
prohibited
spam/overpost
best of craigslist

Free Food

Reply to: sale-399594434@craigslist.org
Date: 2007-08-17, 7:08PM EDT

My father recently passed away and left a stuffy house full of junk. In the basement, we found thousands of cans of food (some from as early as 1920, most from the 1940s) with the labels ripped off. There are mason jars of jam (covered in dust) and pickled meats. There are also jars of water and soured milk. It smells like a sewer down there.

As there are few cans with any labels (I have no idea why he did this), these items have little collectibility and are for consumption only. They're free. Email me for our address. We'll be in town for a couple of weeks cleaning his house out.

* it's NOT ok to contact this poster with services or other commercial interests

PostingID: 399594434

[150 | Wanted: Bear Cubs for My Children]

To: sale-399594434@craigslist.org
Subject: Free Food
Date: Fri, 17 Aug 2007 19:25:45 -0400
From: █████████████

We cleaned an Uncles house out years ago,just like you are and you better look in those jars not labeled!

We did...... and found$560,000

Older people did that alot

Good Luck

To: sale-399594434@craigslist.org
Subject: Free Food
Date: Fri, 17 Aug 2007 16:42:09 -0700
From: █████████████

I'm sorry to hear of your loss. If I can be of any assistance other than eating 60 yr old canned food, let me know. lol.

I dont work and could help clean if you'd like.

████████

To: sale-399594434@craigslist.org
Subject: Free Food
Date: Fri, 16 Aug 2007 16:45:01 -0700 (PDT)
From: █████████████

I am interested in the free food I have six children and they are not picky about what they eat...lol. thanks ████ ████████

email this posting to a friend

please flag with care:
miscategorized
prohibited
spam/overpost
best of craigslist

Free Dildo

Reply to: sale-413220920@craigslist.org
Date: 2007-09-03, 7:08PM EDT

I've had my purple dildo for a couple of years and it's time to retire it.
It still works fine. It's the bullet style, with no strap-on capabilities. It's
not ribbed. Free to whever can come pick it up.

* it's NOT ok to contact this poster with services or other commercial interests

PostingID: 413220920

To: sale-413220920@craigslist.org
Subject: Free Dildo
Date: Mon, 3 Sep 2007 19:46:50 -0700 (PDT)
From: ███████████████

where do you live?

email this posting to a friend

please flag with care:
miscategorized
prohibited
spam/overpost
best of craigslist

Free Pauly Shore cardboard cutout

Reply to: sale-417445271@craigslist.org
Date: 2007-09-08, 3:11PM PDT

Lifesized!! From that movie about when he dates a military man's daughter (can't remember the name). Been sitting in my garage for ten years now and I cant just throw it away!

* it's NOT ok to contact this poster with services or other commercial interests

PostingID: 417445271

To: sale-417445271@craigslist.org
Subject: pauly shore
Date: Sun, 9 Sep 2007 13:02:36 -0700 (PDT)
From: ████████████

I'm sure it's been taken, but if you still have the cardboard Pauly Shore, I REALLY want it.

I can pick it up anytime after work.

COOL!

████

To: sale-417445271@craigslist.org
Subject: Free Pauly Shore cardboard cutout
Date: Sat, 8 Sep 2007 18:53:09 -0700
From: ████████████

HOW MAY IU PICK IT UP?

please flag with care:
miscategorized
prohibited
spam/overpost
best of craigslist

Free Merkins

Reply to: sale-415079839@craigslist.org
Date: 2007-09-05, 11:17PM PDT

My husband is a merkin lover and merkin-making hobbyist. His collection has gotten a bit out of hand lately, and we have to give a bag (or more) away to make room for a treadmill. If you or anyone you know is in need of a merkin, let us know. We have many different styles and colors (including "The Italian," "The Sharon Stone," and "The Heart").

Free for pickup.

* it's NOT ok to contact this poster with services or other commercial interests

PostingID: 415079839

To: sale-415079839@craigslist.org
Subject: free merkins
Date: Thu, 6 Sep 2007 05:11:38 -0700 (PDT)
From: ██████████████

Does he make you wear them

To: sale-415079839@craigslist.org
Subject: Free Merkins
Date: Thu, 6 Sep 2007 02:32:12 -0400
From: ██████████████

WHAT IS A MERKIN?

To: sale-415079839@craigslist.org
Subject: hair
Date: Wed, 5 Sep 2007 21:56:17 -0700 (PDT)
From: ██████████████

I would love to have these merkins!!! Please call me so we can discuss pick up !!! My number is ████████ I live in ██████████ ████....

Thank you - my name is ██████ - ██████████

email this posting to a friend

please flag with care:
miscategorized
prohibited
spam/overpost
best of craigslist

Free Apple G4 Laptop

Reply to: sale-417980695@craigslist.org
Date: 2007-09-09, 2:07PM EDT

OMFG 1 h@v3 7h3 sw3373s7 @ppl3 g4 l@pt0p bu7 my d@d s@ys
1 g00t@ g1v3 1t @w@y bcuz 1 us3 mysp@c3 W@Y 2 MUCH!!!
@n, OMFG LOLZ ROFL 1 t0t@lly d0, bu7 1tz bcuz th3r3s s0 m@ny
H0TT13Z 0N MY FR13NDZ L1S7!!!! LOL, 1 gu3ss 1f u w@n7 1t, u
c@n h@v3 1t bu7 f1rs7 1 g0tt@ g37 @ll my p03mz @b0u7 b0yz 0ff
0f 1t @nd 1 g0tt@ c@ll l1nds@y @nd s33 1f sh3 w@ntz h3r F@LL
0U7 B0Y scr33ns@v3rz 0n @ d1sk. sh3z s0 funny b3cuz sh3 l0v3z
th1s guy n@m3d P@UL bu7 P@UL 1z 1n luv w1t m3, @n why n0t?
1'm th3 s@ss12s7 b1tch ar0und!!! OMG OMG ROFL ROFL ROFL
LOLZ LOLZ !*()U@*PR#

* it's NOT ok to contact this poster with services or other commercial interests

PostingID: 417980695

To: sale-417980695@craigslist.org
Subject: Free Apple G4 Laptop
Date: Sun, 9 Sep 2007 14:31:51 -0400
From: ▮▮▮▮▮▮

Hi I m ▮▮▮▮ and intersty for your laptop pleases send me address and telephone
number for your contacts Tankyou.

▮▮▮▮▮▮▮

email this posting to a friend

please flag with care:
miscategorized
prohibited
spam/overpost
best of craigslist

Free Pontiac Firebird

Reply to: sale-419023659@craigslist.org
Date: 2007-09-10, 2:26PM PDT

So, my son's a total dip. I bought him a Pontiac Firebird and he started beefing it up, taking it on joy rides and racing in parking lots. Well, by the time he turned 19, he had gotten huge on steroids and had a burglary charge against him. And then, the lead witness to the burglary went missing, so he got first-degree murder charges. He told me one night that he would be back for the Firebird, said it was all that mattered to him and that he would find it. He was very serious about keeping the car, as if there was something important about it that he couldn't give up. But then, he left town, and I haven't heard from him in six months.

I want to get this thing out of my driveway. Because it was involved in a crime, and because he's beefed it up with god knows what, I wouldn't feel right selling it. I'm going to give it away to the first person who replies and comes to pick it up. I have the title in hand.

Also, if you've seen my son, please let me know. He's 6'10, bald head, covered with tattoos, big muscles, blue eyes, small nose. He has a tattoo of a spider web on the back of his head and the word "Kriminal" on his chest.

* it's NOT ok to contact this poster with services or other commercial interests

PostingID: 419023659

To: sale-419023659@craigslist.org
Subject: Free Pontiac Firebird
Date: Mon, 10 Sep 2007 14:39:33 -0700
From: ▓▓▓▓▓▓▓▓▓▓▓▓▓

do you think hell shoot me whilst im drivin it????

To: sale-419023659@craigslist.org
Subject: CAR
Date: Mon, 10 Sep 2007 21:38:09 +0000
From: ▓▓▓▓▓▓▓▓▓▓▓▓▓

WHAT IS THE ADDRESS AND YOUR NUMBER SO I CAN CALL YOU FOR
ADDRESS. MY PHONE NUMBER IS ▓▓▓▓▓▓▓▓

To: sale-419023659@craigslist.org
Subject: i would like to keep the car
Date: Mon, 10 Sep 2007 14:40:51 -0700 (PDT)
From: ▓▓▓▓▓▓▓▓▓▓▓▓▓

i would like to keep the car love Pontiac Firebird it on joy rides but i hate racit it in
parking lot or any where, i am a pease men. thanks

email this posting to a friend

Free Pog Collection

Reply to: sale-413222976@craigslist.org
Date: 2007-09-03, 7:37PM PDT

My brother gave me his pog collection when he moved to michigan and I dont want them, but there are plenty of rare and cool ones here such as poisons, 8 balls, skulls, and skateboards. theres even a dodgers slammer and a huge 8ball fire slammer. Theyre all in a box and if no one comes to get them im gonna put them on the curb.

totally free

* it's NOT ok to contact this poster with services or other commercial interests

PostingID: 413222976

To: sale-413222976@craigslist.org
Subject: i want the pogs!!!!
Date: Mon, 03 Sep 2007 20:41:42 -0700
From: ▄▄▄▄▄▄▄▄▄▄▄▄

where do we go to get the righteous pogs bro? here is my number. im ▄▄▄▄

▄▄▄▄▄▄▄▄

please flag with care:
miscategorized
prohibited
spam/overpost
best of craigslist

Bee Gun

Reply to: sale-507679480@craigslist.org
Date: 2007-12-12, 11:25PM EST

The B-1 is an automatic bee rifle capable of firing both single bees and swarms of bees with ease. Developed by local engineering firm Milestone, the B-1 represents a breakthrough in insect-based warfare. Bees are sold flash-frozen and placed within the gun, where they thaw and come to life. The B-1 holds up to a thousand bees, and has three settings: single-fire (in which a single bee is shot), swarm-fire (in which a hundred bees are shot) or hive-fire (in which all one thousand bees are shot). When triggered, the B-1 catapults live bees alongside a spray of honey-water, which coats potential victims.

As this technology is still experimental, we are looking to give away one hundred bee guns to test consumers, who will then fill out a half-page questionnaire after six months of usage. Potential users must provide a small summary of how they would use the bee gun.

The B-1 is slated to retail at $1,999.99.

* it's NOT ok to contact this poster with services or other commercial interests

PostingID: 507679480

To: sale-507679480@craigslist.org
Subject: Bee Gun
Date: Thu, 13 Dec 2007 00:02:42 -0500
From: ███████████████

I would like one\

Please call ███████████

I have a big bee problem here

Chapter 6: For Sale

Lessons I learned in this chapter:

1. Schooners (double-masted sailing vessels) should never be "tricked out."

2. Phil Collins fans are obsessive.

3. Trick fire extinguishers are a tough sell.

email this posting to a friend

please flag with care:
miscategorized
prohibited
spam/overpost
best of craigslist

For sale: Phil Collins wax figure

Reply to: sale-415082257@craigslist.org
Date: 2007-09-05, 10:21PM CDT

My friend is a wax sculptor (he once worked for Md. Tussauds).
For my birthday four years ago he made me a life-sized Phil Collins
(anatomically correct, for anyone wondering!) that looks exactly like
Phil from the No Jacket Required era. I got married six months ago and
my husband can't stand the thing—probably because he knows that I'm
secretly in love with Phil! Anyway, all jokes aside, I have to get rid of
this thing, and I'm willing to do it for pretty cheap.

Make me an offer (can even be next to nothing).

* it's NOT ok to contact this poster with services or other commercial interests

PostingID: 415082257

[164 | Wanted: Bear Cubs for My Children]

To: sale-415082257@craigslist.org
Subject: I must have Phil
Date: Wed, 5 Sep 2007 22:44:34 -0700 (PDT)
From: ███████████████

I am the biggest genesis fan ever..My basement is decked out in rock and roll regalia..It would be sooo cool to have phil sitting or standing at the bar..Pleeezze sell it to me..Please call me tomorrow if you can at ████████.i will definately take him off your hands..thanks alot and ask for ██████..But dont give me "no reply at all" LOL..

To: sale-415082257@craigslist.org
Subject: cards
Date: Thu, 6 Sep 2007 19:39:27 -0700 (PDT)
From: ███████████████

wanna trade for a computer compaq pentium 4

6000 cards

███████

█████████

██████████████

please flag with care:
miscategorized
prohibited
spam/overpost
best of craigslist

Tricked-out seventeenth century schooner

Reply to: sale-507685315@craigslist.org
Date: 2007-12-12, 11:32PM EST

My husband recently inherited a 17th century Dutch schooner from his late father, a notable philanthropist, bibliophile and art collector. The schooner was kept on display in a private Manchester estate, alongside seven other boats of historical relevance. My husband, being the speed freak he is, immediately installed two high-powered, custom-made combustible engines and was "pulled over" by the coast guard within a week. Turns out, he had been drinking (heavily) and was given a B.U.I. Our insurance went through the roof, and I convinced him to sell the boat.

I don't know much about boats, but I do know that the schooner is huge, with several masts, five built-in cannons, and three ancient flags. It also comes with my husband's modifications:

1.) Flames painted on the back.
2.) One of those naked mermaid things on the front.
3.) The name "Bad Boy" painted on the right side in red.
4.) A "skull and bones" pirate sail.
5.) A fully-stocked bar.

Also, this baby is great for waterskiing! It's sure to be the fastest, most unique boat on the water.

* it's NOT ok to contact this poster with services or other commercial interests

PostingID: 507685315

[166 | Wanted: Bear Cubs for My Children]

To: sale-415082257@craigslist.org
Subject: historic vessel ruined by idiot who already lost interest in it
Date: Thu, 13 Dec 2007 12:21:28 -0600
From: ████████████████

If that was a real ad, you guys are a bunch of idiots. to ruin a peice of history like that and turn around and just have it for sale. I come from an old new england seafaring family and value the history of such a thing, you guys must have no sense of tradition, or maybe canadian?

To: sale-415082257@craigslist.org
Subject: Tricked-out seventeenth century schooner
Date: Thu, 13 Dec 2007 13:22:08 -0500
From: ████████████████

Please send pictures of your boat so I may consider a purchase.

What price range are you asking?

Sincerely yours

████.

email this posting to a friend

Li'l' Dictator Toy Set - $10

Reply to: sale-505553802@craigslist.org
Date: 2007-12-10, 11:50PM MST

For sale is a like-new Li'l' Dictator Toy Set. This toy set is for toddlers aged 1-4 years old and is an excellent political learning tool. It comes with one plastic dictator toy, two hundred "follower" toys, twenty dissidents, a "town square" filled with propaganda posters, several tanks, and hundreds of small plastic guns. Within the town square there are button-activated "explosions", wind-up sirens and fake broken glass.

This set is fairly large and would easily entertain two or more children. I've personally watched my young ones act out the rise and fall of fascism and several forms of religious fundamentalism. It's cute.

First ten dollar offer takes it. Makes for a great Christmas or birthday gift.

* it's NOT ok to contact this poster with services or other commercial interests

PostingID: 505553802

[168 | Wanted: Bear Cubs for My Children]

To:	sale-505553802@craigslist.org
Subject:	Li'l' Dictator Toy Set - $10
Date:	Tue, 11 Dec 2007 15:55:10 EST
From:	████████████████████

Do you have a picture of this toy? I am very interested and need a visual if possible. Let me know.

Thanks

████████

email this posting to a friend

please flag with care:
miscategorized
prohibited
spam/overpost
best of craigslist

Trick Fire Extinguisher Blow-Out Sale!!!

Reply to: sale-505548457@craigslist.org
Date: 2007-12-10, 10:40PM PST

Last May, my brother and I started up our own business selling trick fire extinguishers. These extinguishers are the funniest prank you can pull on someone—they look and feel exactly like real extinguishers, but when pulled, emit music and confetti instead of C02. It's hilarious!

We called our joke extinguisher store "Fire Brothers" and went out of business in six weeks. As a result, we have a warehouse full of trick fire extinguishers that we need to liquidate. These would normally retail at $29.99. We've lowered the price to $9.99, with additional sales if purchased in bulk.

The extinguishers come in many models, including:

1.) An extinguisher that shoots candy
2.) An extinguisher that plays "I'm on Fire" by Bruce Springsteen
3.) "Missy Pissy," an extinguisher that ejects a thin stream of yellow water reminiscent of urine
4.) An extinguisher that plays "Burnin' for You" by Blue Öyster Cult
5.) "The Houdini," an extinguisher that, when pulled, begins melting to gas and eventually disappears
6.) An extinguisher that plays "We Didn't Start the Fire" by Billie Joel

* it's NOT ok to contact this poster with services or other commercial interests

PostingID: 505548457

[170 | Wanted: Bear Cubs for My Children]

To: sale-505548457@craigslist.org
Subject: Trick Fire Extinguisher Blow-Out Sale!!!
Date: Wed, 12 Dec 2007 18:06:49 GMT
From: ███████████████

Hi we saw your Craig's Listing for the extinguishers and they are perfect for a co-worker who's always running around with his hair on fire! Do you still have some available, accept pay pal and ship to Arizona? If so, then we would like to get the following ones:

1 - An extinguisher that plays "I'm on Fire" by Bruce Springsteen

1 - An extinguisher that plays "We Didn't Start the Fire" by Billie Joel

1 - An extinguisher that shoots candy

Thanks,

███████████

Chapter 7: Barter

Craigslist is full of bizarre bartering. At the time of this writing, there are people trading cornrow tightening for handyman work, a brown couch for a brake job, a dolphin-shaped alarm clock for a red sofa slipcover, and an orchid for a stamp collection. I wanted to see if someone would trade me their dirty laundry. Almost everyone that replied offered up panties and bras that they'd stolen from someone else—mostly the underwear of their wives or girlfriends.

Go figure.

email this posting to a friend

please flag with care:
miscategorized
prohibited
spam/overpost
best of craigslist

Trade my PS3 for dirty laundry

Reply to: sale-418827584@craigslist.org
Date: 2007-09-10, 2:10PM EDT

I need dirty laundry to smell and enjoy. I'll give my PS3 (almost brand new) for some laundry, but there better be some underwear in there. I don't have any games but it comes with all the connections and two controllers. This is not a joke. I need your laundry.

* it's NOT ok to contact this poster with services or other commercial interests

PostingID: 418827584

To: sale-418827584@craigslist.org
Subject: Trade my PS3 for dirty laundry
Date: Mon, 10 Sep 2007 22:43:00 EDT
From: ███████████████

i am very interested my wife did not do laundrey this week (hot Brown hair big
boobs) i will trade all her laundry (mostly underwear and bras) along with a picture of
her if you wish. i hope you are serious as i am very serious my number is ████████

To: sale-418827584@craigslist.org
Subject: Trade my PS3 for dirty laundry
Date: Mon, 10 Sep 2007 11:53:13 -0700 (PDT)
From: ███████████████

i got what you need.get back asap

To: sale-418827584@craigslist.org
Subject: dirty laundry
Date: Tue, 11 Sep 2007 01:03:35 -0400 (EDT)
From: ███████████████

hi bro. my name is ██████. i have a fat roommate with tons of smelly

 dirty

laundry, this stuff would put down a small horse. i would love a ps3

 for

our dorm.

thanks for your time and i hope to hear back from you soon

Subject: Trade my PS3 for dirty laundry
Date: Sat, 15 Sep 2007 12:43:27 -0400
From: ▊▊▊▊▊▊▊▊▊▊

I have a ton of dirty laundry left behind from my ex-wife. There is underwear, pants, shirts, tons of stuff. I think there might even be some lingerie in there... It's a big trash bag full of stuff. Interested? I'm located in ▊▊▊▊▊▊▊▊, and can deliver. Just shoot me an e-mail. Thanks!

▊▊▊▊▊▊

email this posting to a friend

please flag with care:
miscategorized
prohibited
spam/overpost
best of craigslist

Looking to trade my HD Flat-Screen for a pile of dirt

Reply to: sale-418837634@craigslist.org
Date: 2007-09-10, 1:20PM CDT

I need a pile of dirt for my lawn. I got a Sony SXRD 50 inch HD flat screen tv that I dont use much anymore and if you will deliver me a big pile of dirt its yours. It works just fine and I only got it a couple of months ago but I dont have time to watch tv anymore so Im willing to trade it away.

The dirt needs to be good for an empty lawn and you need to be professional about dropping it off.

* it's NOT ok to contact this poster with services or other commercial interests

PostingID: 418837634

To: sale-418837634@craigslist.org
Subject: Looking to trade my HD Flat-Screen for a pile of dirt
Date: Mon, 10 Sep 2007 16:38:47 EDT
From: ███████████████

STILL LOOKING FOR THAT DIRT? CALL ME I WOULD LOVE TO TRADE

███████

To: sale-418837634@craigslist.org
Subject: Looking to trade my HD Flat-Screen for a pile of dirt
Date: Mon, 10 Sep 2007 14:49:24 -0500
From: ███████████████

Ill by the dirt   send it to your place and get the tv from you

██████ ████████

I'll trade my '69 Mustang for your comic book collection

Reply to: sale-418821275@craigslist.org
Date: 2007-09-10, 2:04PM EDT

Hi there. I've got a large collection of cars and I need to find someone with a comic book collection, because my son is obsessed with them and his birthday is coming up. If you have a nice collection of comics (and I'm going to have to trust you, I don't know the first thing about them), I'll trade you for my '69 Mustang. He's also really into this Magic Gathering card game so if you have some of those to throw in, let me know. My name's Jerry.

She runs just fine. I've kept her in really good shape.

* it's NOT ok to contact this poster with services or other commercial interests

PostingID: 418821275

To: sale-418821275@craigslist.org
Subject: I'll trade my '69 Mustang for your comic book collection
Date: Mon, 10 Sep 2007 14:40:15 -0500
From: ████████████████

Hello: I'll give guitar lessons for that Mustang.

To: sale-418821275@craigslist.org
Subject: Car for comics
Date: Mon, 10 Sep 2007 15:43:57 -0700 (PDT)
From: ████████████████

Hey,

Saw your ad on craigslist, i have old comics that are really old that i can trade you for the car. Do you live anywhere near washington dc?

████████

Chapter 8: Movies

I decided to pen some casting calls for fictitious movies about vampires and explosions, because vampires and explosions seem to be all the American moviegoing public care about anymore. Also included in this chapter are films that feature werewolves, zombies, mermaids, a talking dog, and a "military guy with the fastest car and the biggest guns in the world." To the thousands of unemployed actors who submitted their headshots: keep shooting for the stars!

email this posting to a friend

please flag with care:
miscategorized
prohibited
spam/overpost
best of craigslist

Seeking screenwriters

Reply to: gigs-tjyms-1240161451@craigslist.org
Date: 2009-06-25, 9:10PM PDT

I have to hire two or three writers to help me finish a screenplay that is, without a doubt, the most awful, brainless piece of shit I've ever come across. I've begged my producer to scrap the project, but he refuses. The studio is under the impression that we're going to start shooting sometime next year. Here's the plot so far:

DOG WIZARD is a romantic comedy about a talking dog that is also some sort of wizard. It's supposed to be an action movie, as well, but I'm not sure how. My producer has suggested that we incorporate aliens, vampires, and people in fat suits. He's adamant about the fat suits, but the rest is open for discussion.

That's about all I can tell you about the project. Please send me suggestions on how to tie all of this together.

The pay is lucrative, but you must commit to twenty or thirty hours a week for at least three months.

* it's NOT ok to contact this poster with services or other commercial interests

PostingID: 1240161451

To: gigs-tjyms-1240161451@craigslist.org
Subject: DOG WIZARD
Date: Friday, June 26, 2009 4:14 AM
From: ▮▮▮▮▮▮▮▮▮▮▮▮

Hi,

I'd like to work on your piece of shit screenplay. I've attached my resume. Check out some of my writing (all comedy here) at my ▮▮▮▮▮ page:

▮▮▮

My suggestion is to take all the insane elements that your producer wants to use and run with them. Build some games and patterns out of those elements and heighten the shit out of everything.

Thanks,

▮▮▮▮▮▮▮

email this posting to a friend

please flag with care:
miscategorized
prohibited
spam/overpost
best of craigslist

Casting call for "Werewolf Warriors"

Reply to: gigs-451365054@craigslist.org
Date: 2007-10-16, 8:54PM PDT

WEREWOLF WARRIORS, a new high-budget action flick from Megamonolith Pictures, is holding an open casting call for all roles. Set in the future, WEREWOLF WARRIORS is a martial arts film about werewolf scientists who develop high-tech mechanized robot armor to fight off vampires, mutant humans, and neo-Nazi zombies. After the lead character, LUCIEN, is elected president of the werewolves and kidnapped, war is waged upon the neighboring colonies (Vampirica and China). An evil necromancer, hell-bent on destroying the werewolves, raises an army of undead Third Reich officers. All the while, a mutant race of underground humans (the only survivors of a nuclear holocaust) rise from the sewers, seeking blood.

Filming is slated to take place Spring of 2008. Please reply with a headshot and acting resume.

* it's NOT ok to contact this poster with services or other commercial interests

PostingID: 451365054

[184 | Wanted: Bear Cubs for My Children]

To: gigs-451365054@craigslist.org
Subject: Werewolf Warriors
Date: Tue, 16 Oct 2007 23:46:21 -0700
From: ███████████████

Hi, my name is ██████. I saw your ad on craigslist and thought it sounded great. Here is a link to my headshot because the craigslist bandwidth is to small to attach it ███████████████████████████████████.

The synopsis of this film is awesome. Werewolves are sweet and a highly undervalued horror character and I am glad that someone is producing a film that will have werewoves vs. zombie/undead nazis. I would love to be a part of this film. I recently graduated from the ███████████ and moved out to Los Angeles to become a professional actor. I have always loved film, and have always been drawn to these types of movies. When I was thirteen or so, I would rent horror movies every Tuesday (two for one Tuesdays) and watch them both that night usually. Before that, I used to watch Night of the Living Dead all the time (my parents would let me watch whatever I wanted)

I think this project sounds really special and would be great to be involved with it as an actor. I would love to get more information about this. My phone number is ███████████ or you can reply to this email. I hope to hear from you soon. ███████

To: gigs-451365054@craigslist.org
Subject: Casting call for "Werewolf Warriors"
Date: Wed, 17 Oct 2007 08:14:23 -0700 (PDT)
From: ███████████████

For your consideration: ████████

I'm sending you my "military" face shot. However, I've been the lead zombie in 2 seperate productions. I'm comfortable in the extensive makeup, understand zombie movement and behavior - even zombie "emotion". I would like to submit actual photos from both productions for your consideration, but Craigslist limits the file size. So, if you would like to see them, please provide alternate email, or permission for multiple submission.

Thanks for your time with my resume.

Sincerely, ████████████████

email this posting to a friend

Actors and cast needed for Titanic 2: Mermaid Saviors

Reply to: gigs-505505443@craigslist.org
Date: 2007-12-16, 9:31PM PST

Megamonolith Pictures is holding an open casting call for TITANIC 2: MERMAID SAVIORS, a sequel to the Academy Award-winning 1997 blockbuster TITANIC, on December 15th and 16th. The film begins moments after the sinking of the Titanic. All who have drowned are brought back to life by a futuristic race of mermaids, called the Mantocks, who welcome the humans to their underwater paradise. Soon thereafter, JACK DAWSON is elected king of the underwater humans. DAWSON requests that all humans be returned above water, a request that is denied by KING MANTROCK. The humans are slowly brainwashed into worshiping their mermaid saviors. Meanwhile, the sunken TITANIC has become a haunted underwater wasteland inhabited by RAGGARO and his band of mermaid pirates. Will the humans ever free themselves from their mermaid slavery? Will the mermaid pirates wage war on Mantock?

All actors seeking consideration must reply to this post with:

1.) A headshot and,
2.) A few short paragraphs on why they're qualified for MERMAID SAVIORS.

Actors with mermaid experience are highly desirable.

* it's NOT ok to contact this poster with services or other commercial interests

PostingID: 505505443

[186 | Wanted: Bear Cubs for My Children]

To: gigs-505505443@craigslist.org

Subject: Actors and cast needed for Titanic 2: Mermaid Saviors

Date: Tue, 11 Dec 2007 03:35:01 EST

From: ██████████████████

Hello!

My name is ███████, and I am submitting for your casting, and yes, I do have swim and mermaid experiences.

I thank you for your consideration and hope to have a chance to meet you.

Sincerely,

█████████

To: gigs-505505443@craigslist.org

Subject: Actors and cast needed for Titanic 2: Mermaid Saviors

Date: Mon, 10 Dec 2007 23:56:16 -0800

From: ███████████████████

Name: ████████

Phone: ███████████

I deserve to be pick because I'm a hott young talent actor

~█████████

To: gigs-505505443@craigslist.org
Subject: Actors and cast needed for Titanic 2: Mermaid Saviors
Date: Mon, 10 Dec 2007 22:08:52 -0800
From: ███████████

Professional actress-model

reliable, nice, and easy to work with

no nudity or adult-related work

paid professional assignments only

███████

Why am I qualified for Mermaid Saviors? Well, I should have been born a mermaid because I absolutely love the water! I've been swimming since I was 4 years old and with my long, blond hair and healthy physique, I fit the bill;) Plus, I think that playing a futuristic mermaid would be pretty cool indeed! I'm sure that a colony of mermaids needs a blond or two;)

Thank you

███████

█████████

███████████████

Extras needed for summer blockbuster

Reply to: gigs-tjyms-1240156155@craigslist.org
Date: 2009-06-25, 8:40PM PDT

EXPLOSION – THE MOVIE! is casting extras for pivotal explosion scenes.

Plot synopsis: a series of mysterious explosions occur around the globe, each more exciting and explosive than the last.

We've already filmed scenes involving explosions of gas refineries, pillow factories, hog farms, abandoned warehouses, elementary schools, racetracks, football stadiums, and national monuments.

Extras will stand at a safe distance from the explosions and then, after the explosions, panic. Pay is $1,000 a day. Please respond with daytime availability and, if applicable, relevant film work.

* it's NOT ok to contact this poster with services or other commercial interests

PostingID: 1240156155

To: gigs-tjyms-1240156155@craigslist.org
Subject: Also
Date: Friday, June 26, 2009 3:56 AM
From: ▮▮▮▮▮▮▮▮▮▮

My number is ▮▮▮▮▮▮. I am very interested, in good shape, and can run around
and don't mind explosions. Feel free to contact me whenever.

Thanks,

▮▮▮▮▮▮

To: gigs-tjyms-1240156155@craigslist.org
Subject: Extras
Date: Friday, June 26, 2009 6:22 AM
From: ▮▮▮▮▮▮▮▮▮▮

Hello,

   I am available during the day from 11-5 and i don't have any film work experience
but I do know how to panic. So if I can be of assistance please contact me asap.

Sincerely,

▮▮▮▮▮▮▮

▮▮▮▮▮

To: gigs-tjyms-1240156155@craigslist.org
Subject: Fw: Resume
Date: Friday, June 26, 2009 9:56 AM
From: ▮▮▮▮▮▮▮▮▮▮

HI MY NAME IS ▮▮▮▮▮ AND MY CELL IS ▮▮▮▮▮▮. MY AVAILABILITY IS
OPEN ANYTIME RIGHT NOW.

To: gigs-tjyms-1240156155@craigslist.org
Subject: Explosions Extra!
Date: Friday, June 26, 2009 4:42 PM
From: ████████████████

I want to see stuff blow up! Available all day ASAP. Resume is attached.

Thanks,

████████████

Headshot available upon request.

email this posting to a friend

please flag with care:
miscategorized
prohibited
spam/overpost
best of craigslist

Casting call for action film

Reply to: gigs-p5swq-1240167431@craigslist.org
Date: 2009-06-25, 11:52PM PDT

Megamonolith Pictures is proud to present a casting call for THE MILITARY GUY WITH THE FASTEST CAR AND THE BIGGEST GUNS IN THE WORLD WHO IS CONSTANTLY FLIRTING WITH DEATH AND SLAUGHTERING BAD GUYS BUT WHO IS, AT HEART, A GOOD PERSON THAT WANTS TO RAISE HIS KIDS RIGHT AND AVENGE THE DEATH OF HIS WIFE WHO WAS KILLED BY TERRORISTS THAT HAVE INFILTRATED THE WHITE HOUSE AND TAKEN THE PRESIDENT HOSTAGE AND WHO ARE DEMANDING THE CODES TO A SECRET NUCLEAR ARSENAL BUT WHO WILL ULTIMATELY DIE BY THE HAND OF THE MILITARY GUY WITH THE FASTEST CAR AND THE BIGGEST GUNS IN THE WORLD BECAUSE HE IS THE ULTIMATE KILLING MACHINE (working title).

We're seeking to fill the roles of PRIMARY VILLAIN, SEX INTEREST, and HENCHMAN 1 and 2. These are union jobs and will involve six months of work in Los Angeles and Venezuela.
PRIMARY VILLAIN: a sneaky, sadistic, bearded lunatic who always kills everyone in sight.
SEX INTEREST: A buxom blonde incapable of doing anything but screaming and being kidnapped.
HENCHMAN 1: Large and mentally challenged meathead.
HENCHMAN 2: Large and slightly less mentally challenged meathead.

Please send headshots and previous film experience.

* it's NOT ok to contact this poster with services or other commercial interests

PostingID: 1240167431

[192 I Wanted: Bear Cubs for My Children]

To: gigs-p5swq-1240167431@craigslist.org
Subject: Casting call for action film
Date: Friday, June 26, 2009 11:58 AM
From: ████████████

Hello. I'm a SAG actor submitting my headshot and resume in consideration of auditioning for the role of the 'Primary Villain' in the upcoming Film. I have no objections to growing a beard. Feel free to contact me with any questions or concerns.

A direct link to my headshot and resume is as follows: ████████████████████
████████

Thank you,

████████

████████████

████████████

To: gigs-p5swq-1240167431@craigslist.org
Subject: Casting call for action film
Date: Friday, June 26, 2009 12:53 PM
From: ████████████

I am willing to play the sex interest, let me know if you want me for the part, see more pictures and videos at the links on my resume, myspace.com, youtube.com, and flickr.com, copy and paste links, have the most content on them. Contact me if you want to hire me.

████████

To: gigs-p5swq-1240167431@craigslist.org
Subject: Casting call for action film
Date: Friday, June 26, 2009 4:55 PM
From: ██████████████

Hi, my name is ██████ and I provide picture cars. Have you decided what the fastest car that this military guy drives is? I'm an experienced professional and have worked with many companies, So far this year I've worked ██████████. Currently I'm working on ██████████, which is being directed by ██████████████. I specialize in ██████████████, but of course I can get anything. Best, ██████

Chapter 9: Random

Lessons learned in this chapter:

1. People who fashion bongs out of plastic Jesus dolls are "going to hell."

2. Kegs filled with bible water are in no way popular or desirable.

3. Live action role playing is equally unpopular and undesirable.

email this posting to a friend

Wanted: Some Advice (My Wife is Fat)

Reply to: comm-401147877@craigslist.org

Date: 2007-08-19, 11:47PM EST

Hey guys, I really need some advice. My wife is just plain fat. When we got married she was a fox. We had two kids, and now she just sits around the house and eats candy all day. I told her a few times last week that she needed to start working out again and to stop with all the soda. She just cried and kept on stuffing her face.

I just don't think it's very fair. If I'd have known that she was going to get like this, I might have reconsidered marrying her. I mean, there should be some sort of agreement, like a prenup, stating that the wife will never get fat. Am I right? Because now, what am I going to do? I'm gonna work a 9 to 5 for the next forty years so this cow can sit at home and eat her chocolate cake. Come on. That's just not fair.

So what do you think I should do? Is there anything I can do? I just want my hot wife back. Not too much to ask, right?

* it's NOT ok to contact this poster with services or other commercial interests

PostingID: 401147877

To: comm-401147877@craigslist.org
Subject: wife is fat?
Date: Mon, 27 Aug 2007 07:10:24 +0300
From: ████████████████

have you found a solution to help your wife get back in shape? i'd love to hear your advice

---

To: comm-401147877@craigslist.org
Subject: Wanted: Some Advice (My Wife is Fat)
Date: Mon, 20 Aug 2007 01:49:52 -0400
From: ████████████

HI!

Well, I'm not a guy and yes, you might ask to much!!! Sure, I'm fat, even I wasn't, you would think of that , right? So don't bother to ask.

Ask this! Why is she stuffing her with candies?

Well, she need some love. Sugar is love. Yeah , baby!! She misses it and if no one around to give her love and affection and devotion, she help herself. And who's fault she miss love? Of course. Yours! :)

Be logical and find a good way for both of you and help her. I bet she does not like herself either that much.

good luck,

████████████

please flag with care:
miscategorized
prohibited
spam/overpost
best of craigslist

ROLE PLAYERS NEEDED FOR Massive Vampire: The Masquerade LARP

Reply to: comm-396442416@craigslist.org
Date: 2007-08-13, 10:20PM PDT

Needed: Experienced RP'ers for massive Vampire: The Masquerade live action role-playing in a field by my stepdad's house. I am a lovely Toreador (Beatrix) who wears a silk sash and cool leather pants. We've got five Malkavians, three Tremeres, seven Gangrels and six others (they're undecided as to which character they're going to bring to our festival). We've done this before but there may be over twenty people there and i'm not going to be the only girl this time (we have like at least seven). And this guy Derek told me what the story is about (its really twisted and i'll only tell you if you email me).

We want this to happen every other week. If you send me a copy of your character sheet, I'll write you into the storyline. We have all kinds of props and my mom's going to make these awesome jalapeno poppers (she's really cool).

I swear this is going to be so effing sweet. And if you want, we can try to put together some sort of D&D thing too.

* it's NOT ok to contact this poster with services or other commercial interests

PostingID: 396442416

Subject: Masquerade

Date: Thu, 16 Aug 2007 14:27:31 -0400

From: ███████████████

Wow that sounds really cool, I love this game...

I've never played any live action before though, how does it work?

Could you tell me about the story too? Also I'm curious...

What kind of age group is this, the part about your mom making food kinda threw me off, is alcohol allowed?

thanks!

please flag with care:
miscategorized
prohibited
spam/overpost
best of craigslist

$100 / 5br - Five Bedroom House

Reply to: hous-39641329@craigslist.org
Date: 2007-08-16, 3:33PM EDT

Alright I got this big house that used to be really nice but a family moved in six months ago and screwed it all up. It was really clean when they signed the lease, but they must have had a zoo come through because there was poop everywhere. All different kinds, and the neighbors said they seen pigs and sheep and other larger animals running around in the lawn from time to time. Also, them kids was living in filth because the parents used my floors as a trash bin.

I cleaned it as best I could but there's still stains all over the place and it smells. . . better, but still bad. There's a bit of a pest problem because of all the trash they left behind. Theres a bunch of leaks in the roof and there's mold in the basment. I did the best I could to make it hospitable but I'm moving soon, so what you see is what you get. That's why its only a hundred a month, when before I was charging 2000.

Other problems:
* holes in the walls * water brown from time to time * lawn dead * foundation rotted * was abandoned for a while, so theres some graffiti on the walls * may be haunted, not sure if that really exists

Benefits:
* CHEAP!!! * comes with a piano and a pet snake * month to month lease * no deposit

* it's NOT ok to contact this poster with services or other commercial interests

PostingID: 39641329

[200 | Wanted: Bear Cubs for My Children]

To: hous-398641329@craigslist.org
Subject: your house...I want to see it please!!!
Date: Tue, 21 Aug 2007 13:47:56 -0700
From: ███████████████

Hi!!

My name is ███████. i saw your ad on craigslist.

Your place does not sound that bad to me. I just moved to Miami from a job corps in Missouri. Plus i've had a few roomates since I got here that sound about like that. the only difference is that their place was smaller.

As long as their is working ac, a fridge, the ghost doesn't go all rose red movie on me, the snake doesn't devour me in my sleep, and the floor doesn't collapse we're all good.

I'd like to here from you on htis as soon as possible. Weird right? You don't know where I'm at now!!! Please call me at ███████████ or email me at

███████████████████████

Thanks bunches,

███████████

email this posting to a friend

Seeking the Ultimate Shredder

Reply to: comm-417414201@craigslist.org
Date: 2007-09-08, 4:27PM EDT

Dudes, we're starting an epic rock band and me and doug wanna find the best guitar shredder in all of Dallas. Influences include Malmsteen, Maiden, Sabbath and Queen. We got a drummer a singer a bass player and another guitarist but we need a lead guitarist who can MAKE FIRE WITH HIS FINGERS! Theres a few songs already, ones called "The walk" and another one we just call "Hot Jam 2" because hot jam 1 was something we scrapped (it was a reggae song that this dude named Kelly wrote before he moved to Baton Rouge).

Theres plenty of room for solos in these songs and we already have a bunch of connections for shows and recording. You just need to reply with why youre the ultimate shredder and maybe a clip of you playing or something.

Peace out.

* it's NOT ok to contact this poster with services or other commercial interests

PostingID: 417414201

To: comm-417414201@craigslist.org
Subject: shredder
Date: Sat, 8 Sep 2007 17:06:49 -0700 (PDT)
From: ███████████████

███████ This song I wrote is called ████████████. It shows that I can thrash, bash, shred and make dead. Look around a little because I have around 30 songs/ clips posted. I'm very versatile, meaning I can play just about anything you throw in front of me, with practice, of course. I don't think I have any songs on there with many arpeggios but I can do at least simple arpeggios at high speeds. I have a half stack and 2 guitars, a noise gate, and a 10 band equalizer. I don't really like using very many FX because I don't rely on them to sound like I'm breathing fire. Anyway, I live in ████████████ and my name is █████████. You can either reply to this or hit my cell at ██████████. Looking forward to hearing from you.

email this posting to a friend

please flag with care:

miscategorized

prohibited

spam/overpost

best of craigslist

I am looking to get into alcoholism

Reply to: comm-455786451@craigslist.org
Date: 2007-10-21, 9:25PM EDT

I've been kicking around the idea of getting into alcoholism for a couple of months. I've decided that I want to try it out and see where it takes me. My father was a big drinker and it left him penniless. I want to prove to the world that you can be an alcoholic and still keep a job and a healthy family.

If you could help me out with this dream, I would appreciate it. I'm looking for a few people to give me some advice on how to go about becoming an alcoholic. You would be willing to show me the "tricks of the trade" and spend about a week mentoring me on how to be the best alcoholic I can possibly be. I'll pay you a couple hundred dollars for your time.

* it's NOT ok to contact this poster with services or other commercial interests

PostingID: 455786451

To: comm-455786451@craigslist.org

Subject: now this is interesting......

Date: Mon, 22 Oct 2007 09:48:53 -0700 (PDT)

From: ███████████████████

hello, personal assistant here!! so you want to be an alchy huh?? very easy,but my advice doesnt come for free....drinking heavily can be alot of fun!! i would recommend some transportation,because you dont want to end up in jail!! you can flirt aimlessly,make people laugh,have loads of fun,go to work totally hung over..... HEY MESSAGE ME!!

email this posting to a friend

please <u>flag</u> with care:
<u>miscategorized</u>
<u>prohibited</u>
<u>spam/overpost</u>
<u>best of craigslist</u>

Bible Kegger!

Reply to: <u>comm-505535298@craigslist.org</u>
Date: 2007-12-11, 1:18AM EST

At Light of Christ Christian Church, we pride ourselves on our BIBLE KEGGERS!!! Every month, we fill a keg with premium holy water and get CRAZY! And we want you to join us! This Friday, December 14th, we're having us an open kegger. There'll be bible trivia, duck duck goose, volleyball and, as always, a keg of non-alcoholic holy water. Come get buzzed on Christ!

* it's NOT ok to contact this poster with services or other commercial interests

PostingID: 505535298

To: comm-505535298@craigslist.org
Subject: Bible Kegger!
Date: Thu, 13 Dec 2007 11:22:17 -0800
From: ████████████████

Hi there, I'm a reporter with ████████████████ who saw this ad on Craigslist. I must say that this sounds like a very unusual kegger! Can someone tell me more?

Sincerely,

████████

████████████

[206 | Wanted: Bear Cubs for My Children]

please flag with care:
miscategorized
prohibited
spam/overpost
best of craigslist

Wanted: A Blowtorch

Reply to: sale-402895145@craigslist.org
Date: 2007-08-21, 8:29PM PDT

I can't take it anymore.

* it's NOT ok to contact this poster with services or other commercial interests

PostingID: 402895145

To: sale-402895145@craigslist.org
Subject: Craigslist wanted ad
Date: Wed, 22 Aug 2007 00:04:25 -0700 (PDT)
From: ▇▇▇▇▇▇▇▇▇▇▇

Hi there

I saw your ad "Wanted: A Blowtorch" on craigslist. You know you could probably get it on eBay. Check this site out:

▇▇▇▇▇▇▇▇▇▇▇▇▇▇▇▇▇▇▇▇▇▇▇▇▇▇▇▇

Hope this helps

▇▇▇▇▇

email this posting to a friend

please flag with care:

miscategorized

prohibited

spam/overpost

best of craigslist

Lost: Nativity Baby Jesus

Reply to: comm-507689300@craigslist.org
Date: 2007-12-12, 10:37AM CST

Anybody seen my baby Jesus bong? One minute, I'm smoking out of the thing and the next, POOF. Kaput. Nowhere to be found.

I guess I should tell you what it looks like. So, last winter, me and my buddy Jer went around stealing baby Jesuses from lawn nativity scenes. Most of them came from churches. We decided to make a bong out of this one, because it was huge and the baby Jesus looked totally stoned. Jer's really good at making bongs, so I left it up to him. He drilled a hole in the baby Jesus' head and put a stem where his penis was, and the thing hit like a champ.

Now I can't find it. I remember taking it to the park last week. It's made out of plastic.

Did you find it at the park?

* it's NOT ok to contact this poster with services or other commercial interests

PostingID: 507689300

To: comm-507689300@craigslist.org
Subject: Lost: Nativity Baby Jesus
Date: Thu, 13 Dec 2007 12:47:45 -0800 (PST)
From: ▓▓▓▓▓▓▓▓▓▓▓▓▓▓▓

Wow your a loser. And your going to hell bitch.

[208 | Wanted: Bear Cubs for My Children]

Chapter 10: Flagged

One of the most interesting and bewildering powers of the craigslist community is the ability to flag posts. If enough users flag a post, it's automatically taken down. This happened to me no less than a hundred times. The problem became quickly apparent: if my posts were too obvious or too offensive, they were flagged. In some cases, I thought the material was too good to discard, and I've included it here.

email this posting to a friend

please flag with care:
miscategorized
prohibited
spam/overpost
best of craigslist

Free iPhone skull grafts

Reply to: <u>sale-505533665@craigslist.org</u>
Date: 2007-12-11, 12:14AM CST

At Morning/Williams Inc., we've spent the greater part of a decade studying cell phone technologies, as well as the correlation between cell phone usage and brain tumors. Thus, we can say with all honesty and confidence that it is not only possible to have a cell phone grafted to your skull... it's convenient and free! And this month, we're screening applicants for FREE IPHONES. Potential applicants must be between the ages of 21 and 45 and in good health.

If you are chosen as a tester, we will provide you with a FREE IPHONE skull graft. This means that an iPhone will be fused to the surface of your skull and connected to your brain, wherein synapses will send graphical images to your visual cortex, allowing you to view your music collection, access your GMail, and text message. Due to the highly experimental nature of this FREE IPHONE, all test subjects must sign wavers before being grafted.

So get rid of those pesky ear-mounted blue tooth devices. This little baby's goin' INSIDE YOUR HEAD. What could be more convenient?

* it's NOT ok to contact this poster with services or other commercial interests

PostingID: 505533665

[210 I Wanted: Bear Cubs for My Children]

email this posting to a friend

please flag with care:

miscategorized

prohibited

spam/overpost

best of craigslist

Mad scientist seeking rival mad scientist for science war

Reply to: comm-505490817@craigslist.org
Date: 2007-12-11, 12:10AM EST

Greetings evil science wizards! Mad scientist here, desiring another mad scientist for a good old-fashioned science duel. I've been holed up in my laboratory, putting the finishing touches on several brilliant inventions, including the Colterhammer (an instrument used to drill into the earth's core), the Whylier (a cruel torture device) and the Hobbler (a sound weapon capable of inflicting paralysis). Dare you step up to my mighty Tivenlarber (a time machine that pulls terrifying prehistoric animals from their natural habitats and places them at the feet of my enemies)? How would you like a taste of my Kilkometer (a raygun that reorganizes the molecular makeup of its target)? Or a dose of Dwarf medicine (a liquid that causes miniaturization)? I think not!

I urge you, fellow mad scientists, to bring it! Our science war will take place in the town square, surrounded by awe-stricken villagers and the mayor himself! Or, in the food court! My friend Jerry works at the Orange Julius there!

Have you the courage to challenge a legend and triumph, I'll offer you my kingdom. This includes my duplex, my cats, my Trek DVD's, my library, and yes... MY COVETED LABORATORY!

* it's NOT ok to contact this poster with services or other commercial interests

PostingID: 505490817

email this posting to a friend

please flag with care:
miscategorized
prohibited
spam/overpost
best of craigslist

Chocolate-Covered Pistols

Reply to: sale-507682720@craigslist.org
Date: 2007-12-12, 11:29PM EST

I have a fresh batch of chocolate-covered pistols for sale, fresh out of the oven. These have always been a holiday treat in our household, and make for beautiful stocking stuffers. They're dipped in high-quality Godiva chocolate and baked with the utmost care, then loaded with chocolate-covered bullets and frozen. The result is a delicious—and explosive!—treat.

I'm selling a half-dozen for $250, or a baker's dozen for $400.

A perfect gift for chocolate lovers and hunters alike!

* it's NOT ok to contact this poster with services or other commercial interests

PostingID: 507682720

[212 | Wanted: Bear Cubs for My Children]

email this posting to a friend

please flag with care:
miscategorized
prohibited
spam/overpost
best of craigslist

free my sister

Reply to: sale-398144600@craigslist.org
Date: 2007-08-15, 7:45PM MST

Mom wont let me give casey away but im gon ta do it nyway so send me this email and i will

she wont now that caseys gon becuse shes sleeping and shes alwayas drunk and paul left her a monthago

* it's NOT ok to contact this poster with services or other commercial interests

PostingID: 398144600

please flag with care:

miscategorized

prohibited

spam/overpost

best of craigslist

WANTED: Private Detective

Reply to: sale-399643449@craigslist.org
Date: 2007-08-17, 5:20PM PDT

Here's how it played out. Me and Skinny were down at Jimmy's Roadside dive with a coupl' a chippies throwing die. Mel C comes in and says that Big Paul got the rub-out. I snuffed my gasper out and raced to Skinny's T-Bird. We took the coastal back to our hideout and sang the who's-and-what's. If Paul had gotten the Harlem Sunset, it meant the other side had heard. And if they'd heard, we had a rat. The kind of rat that turns his whispers to gold. The worst kind.

So here's where you come in, kid. I've got a list of people we need tailed. I've got a lipstick kiss on a napkin with an out of town phone number. And I've got a syndicate breathing down my back. In other words, I've got crumb.

You need to be the kind of shamus who can turn crumb into Thanksgiving dinner.

* it's NOT ok to contact this poster with services or other commercial interests

PostingID: 399643449

email this posting to a friend

Hell Stallion Up for Adoption

please flag with care:
miscategorized
prohibited
spam/overpost
best of craigslist

Reply to: comm-505543133@craigslist.org
Date: 2007-12-11, 12:30AM CST

I've got a certified hell stallion up for adoption. We found her in a lake of blood frothing maggots from the sides of her mouth. She's known to shoot fire from her eyes and occasionally runs faster than time. She's the perfect gift for a young girl or an evil sword-wielding madman who lacks a conscience. We named her "Muffins" but you're free to change it. She'll need a steady supply of fresh blood and carrots, as well as immunizations and a few acres to roam. Adoption fee is fifty dollars, and that includes an iron saddle, golden shoes and an amulet with Latin inscriptions. New owners must be tolerant of random pyrokinesis, rifts in the space-time continuum, and apocalyptic visions.

She has the cutest little chin and loves to be petted on her head between the bone spikes and the flame Mohawk. Also, she's great at jumping obstacles and torturously screaming until the sky turns black. Adopters take note: "Muffins" is not a sociable hell mare and must be kept alone. Any attempts at breeding will result in a half-man, half-horse hybrid, which will certainly kill any human it lays eyes upon.

We've been told by a vet that she's at least 450 years old. She needs an expert rider. No beginners, please. The adoption fee does not include delivery.

* it's NOT ok to contact this poster with services or other commercial interests

PostingID: 505543133